The Why Force for Leaders

The Why Force for Leaders

ISBN 978-1-914209-06-2

eISBN 978-1-914209-07-9

Published in 2021 by Flying Squad Books

© Jerry Hopkins 2021

The right of Jerry Hopkins to be identified as the author of this work has been asserted in accordance with the Copyright, Designs and Patents Act 1988. A CIP record of this book is available from the British Library.

All rights reserved. No part of this book may be reproduced, stored in a retrieval system, or transmitted in any form or by any means, electronic, mechanical, photocopying, recording or otherwise, without the prior written permission of the copyright holder. No responsibility for loss occasioned to any person acting or refraining from action as a result of any material in this publication can be accepted by the author or publisher.

The Why Force for Leaders

JERRY HOPKINS

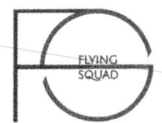

Contents

Luck	7
1. Think	11
2. Back to Basics	15
3. The End	21
4. Less Is More	29
5. New Skills	33
6. The Infinite Cycle	39
7. Rock Time	43
8. Team Why	49
9. Team Values	53
10. Right People	59
11. TOP Planning	63
12. The Weekly 60	69
13. 1P-121 Tool	75
14. Engaging Jobs	81
15. Icing the Cake	85
16. Simply the Best	89
Acknowledgements	93
Work with Jerry	95

Luck

Have you ever noticed how some people seem to achieve more than others? I am not talking about financially, but that might also be so. I am talking in terms of the richness of their lives, their sense of fulfilment and their contribution to the communities they are in. It might be someone you admire, a close friend or family member or yourself. It's easy to think that they or yourself are in some way 'blessed'... more so than others. However, for the vast majority of people, their life's richness, their success and their achievements are purely down to how well they access, both personally and in teams they lead, a resource that is freely available to us all.

In his 1962 book *Gary Player's Golf Secrets,* Player tells an anecdote about his fellow golfer Jerry Barber, a great sand player, who was practising bunker shots. He hit one ball near the flag. The next shot went in. A person watching Jerry told him: 'Gee, you sure are a lucky trap shot player.' 'Yes, I know,' Jerry replied. 'And the harder I practise, the luckier I get.' This quote went on to be attributed to many golfers, including Player himself, and may not even have been first said by Jerry Barber.

In 1974, Greg Lake (of Emerson, Lake & Palmer) recorded the song 'I believe in Father Christmas' as a protest song about the commercialisation of Christmas. It was at a time of protest against the government too, and an adaptation of Thomas Jefferson's (or Joseph De Maestri's) quote 'the government you elect is the government you deserve' was originally intended to be included. Thinking that was too depressing, Lake changed it to the now famous line 'Hallelujah! Noel!, be it Heaven or Hell, the Christmas we get, we deserve.'

Luck, and a four-letter word meaning something close to the opposite of luck, happens. You could win the lottery or be hit by a bus while sipping from a water fountain after a tai chi lesson, but it is perhaps one of the worst traps someone can fall into, to rely on it or fear it. What is more important is how we go about putting ourselves in a position where what others might perceive as good luck comes our way and where what might be perceived as bad luck is less likely to happen. Then it is a case of what we do when opportunities come our way and what action we take in the face of adversity.

So, on average, it probably goes without saying – but say it anyway I will! – that we make our own luck and we get what we deserve as individuals. But the same goes for the other level we operate at: in teams. We are all in multiple teams whether they are family teams, business teams, organisational teams, teams of friends, charity teams, religious teams, sports teams, supporting teams, marriages… the list goes on. Teams again, on average, make their own luck, but one member of the team tends to have more influence than others and that person is the leader. In some teams, particularly family ones – but it is often the case in businesses too – there can be multiple leaders, which can somewhat hamper progress if there is no agreement on direction and actions to be taken among them.

Gerry Robinson, who used to run Granada Television, did a television series and then wrote a book called *I'll Show Them Who's Boss*. It presents the argument that for most teams to succeed, you do need a single leader and it is no accident that most corporations have a single CEO or managing director. It is absolutely not the case that the leader has to have all the ideas… in fact, somewhat the opposite, and you do not want the kind of team where everyone falls prey to groupthink and just agrees with each other or the leader. But ultimately too many chiefs is not a good thing and you see this hamper the progress of organisations like hospitals, law and accounting partnerships, some sports teams and sometimes families. This book will assume that you are the leader of a team – not necessarily the whole organisation, but at least a fairly autonomous unit.

There is a story that when Bill Gates and Warren Buffett first met at a dinner hosted by Mary Gates, she asked them if they believed there was a single factor most instrumental in their success. They both gave the same one-word answer: 'Focus'. It is absolutely the case that every successful person and team needs to be focused, but lots of unsuccessful people and teams are also focused… focused on the wrong things. So, it is actually a two-part process: as individuals and as teams, we first have to determine what our purpose or our 'Why' is. It is this Why that is behind the title of this book. Once we know this, we then need to focus all our energy and resources on achieving it.

When you know your Why as both an individual and as a team and are focused on it as an individual and a team, you will actually feel unnaturally lucky. This is because something medically called 'The Reticular Activating System' will kick in for you. It is like when you buy a new car, you notice other people seem to have suddenly done so. Well, they have not, you are just now more focused on that make, brand or colour of car. It is the same when you know your Why and are focused on it, you notice the things that would have otherwise passed you by, be it a conversation, something you see on the internet, a person with a particular skill, etc. It feels strange how 'lucky' you have suddenly become with this strange force working in your favour. Until you get used to and recognise it for what it is… your Why or 'The Why Force' working for you every day.

It is as easy as that… just determine your individual and team Why and focus on it. But, unfortunately, it is not and it is definitely not a good idea to rush into to determining what your Why is too early. For individuals, you probably will not get close to determining this until well into your thirties and for organisations it can take several years to figure it out (very few organisations start with what the Why is that brings them success). And then the world will conspire to distract you and you will even distract yourself, so many people and teams find the focusing part to be a little more complex than it sounds!

All this means we have to do something that most people and teams are not very good at… THINK! Your ability to carve out quality thinking time to be clear on what you are about, then focus on it and act towards it, will determine how successful, not lucky, you are as an individual and a team… the team you lead. So, that is where we will start our journey.

1 Think

At some point in our lives, we have all heard (possibly screamed at us) and used (possibly screamed at someone else) the expression 'I can't hear myself think'. On examination, it seems like one that does not make sense, but it is referencing that all-important 'inner voice' we all have. To connect with and focus your energy on your Personal Why you need to carve out quality thinking time. Those who practise meditation or mindfulness will already know the huge benefits of doing so, but, even if those two words jar with you, please do not be put off. This is the number one habit both in terms of order and importance that you need to get into... so absolutely no skipping over this and saying that you will find some time to think while hurtling to work each morning! The key thing is that it has to be quality thinking time and it has to be every day... miss a day and then you'll miss two, and before you know it you are moving towards where you need to be at a far slower pace than you could be. We are talking about finding somewhere between two and five minutes each day. Everyone has this time. Don't believe yourself for a second (that you don't have) if you feel you don't!

So, a couple of 'rules' on what is quality thinking time and what is not:

1. You have to be alone and free from distractions. So it cannot be at a time when a dependant needs you, you are concentrating on driving, are in a busy train carriage, are sitting at your desk with your emails open or your phone on, have a dog tugging at your sleeve, are eating your muesli or are listening to the radio or television.
If you live in a very busy household, this might involve getting up before everyone else or sitting in your car for five minutes before going into your place of work.

11

2. You need to be able to look at notes and previous actions that you have made before and be able to write down actions you are going to take, preferably directly into whatever system you use to track actions. If you want all your thoughts and notes to be on a computer, tablet or phone, you will need that device with you, but with all email and messaging turned off.

WARNING: This is not a drill! It is not like some New Year's resolution that does not even outlast the hangover (maybe that's just me!). It is something you need to make a commitment with yourself that you will do forever. It is the cornerstone of what will accelerate firstly yourself and then the team you lead towards achieving your respective purposes and then sustaining doing so.

So, what is that time for you? It may be different on different days of the week (like the weekends). Write it down or put it directly into your diary (just five minutes per day maximum). Is writing it down or putting it in your diary enough to guarantee you do so? Be honest with yourself. If not, what other action do you need to take to make sure you do? It could involve telling someone else you are close to. A bit like when you get sponsorship to run a marathon, telling others can often help hold yourself to doing so. It can also help with the second question, which is: what do you need to do to guarantee that you will not be distracted during that time? I would advise also putting up some sort of sign, turning off phones, definitely turning off emails, etc. So, go ahead now and put your plan in place... Remember, it is a commitment forever, even if at a later date you change the timings as circumstances change.

Now you ask, 'What do I do with this time?' A good question, given that you may not have a strong sense yet of your Personal Why. We will be coming on to this quite soon, so do not worry too much about that. For now, just use the time to do two things that all successful people do.

First, think of an action that you can definitely do that day that will take you one small step closer to any goals that you currently have in your mind or written down. The smaller the step, the better and, if it involves other people, even better too. Successful

1: THINK

people are constantly taking proactive steps towards their goals, so start developing this habit from today, even if you are not too certain of where you want to get to yet.

The second thing I want you to do is make sure that you have something planned that is a 'Beacon'. This is something that you are going to absolutely love doing later that day. It could be:

➤ a game you will play

➤ time with friends

➤ reading a book

➤ doing a puzzle

➤ preparing a lovely meal

➤ watching a particular series

... anything that will totally make your heart sing when you are doing it. Make a list now of all the things that you could select as a Beacon that could pretty much be done any day. You need to have enough so you can definitely have one in place every day.

Again, successful people sustain their energy and having something that they are going to love doing at some point during the day is key to this.

That's it for now: just think for two to five minutes every day, decide on one small step toward one thing you want to achieve and make sure you have a Beacon to look forward to that day. We will soon start to develop further how you use this time, but DO NOT let it slip. Next up we will be considering how most people have more time and money than they realise... so that's good news!

2 Back to Basics

It is important in this chapter to first put things in perspective. The chart below from Our World in Data shows the percentage of people living in extreme poverty over the last 200 years.

Source: ourworldindata.org/extreme-poverty

The actual numbers are 89.15% (in 1820) and 9.98% (in 2015). There are around 7.8 billion of us currently, so 780 million people live on less than $1.90 per day. In 1820, world population was about 1 billion, so 900 million lived in extreme poverty. On the one hand, that means a lot more people are not in extreme poverty; on the other hand, a similar number overall are still in that situation.

The Why-Force for Leaders

The point is that I suspect that neither you nor pretty much anyone you know really lives on a cliff edge where a small piece of bad luck is going to tip you over. In fact, if you look at a version of Abraham Maslow's well-known hierarchy of needs:

- ➤ Our first need, **food**: to eat, drink and survive, which means having a job or a dependable income enough to buy the things we need to keep our bodies going. This is fairly well taken care of and we are not living through a famine.

- ➤ Our second need, **shelter**: to be safe with a roof over our heads and be in a healthy state. Again, this is pretty much taken care of and most of us are not living in a war zone.

- ➤ Our third need, **tribe**: to not have social threats where we are about to lose friends and key relationships, which in prehistoric times would have meant almost certain death. Again, this is for most people at least good enough... for now!

- ➤ And finally our fourth need, **meaning**: feeling a sense of purpose and achievement to fulfil our psychological and spiritual needs. This will again be taken care of to a certain extent, but most people have a nagging doubt that they could be doing more with their lives... and they are probably right.

Most of us are not fighting for survival... unless we are one of the relatively few people who are in an accident or are struck by a serious illness that is not related to old age. So, most of us actually have a huge amount of choice... in fact, an infinite amount of choice unless you believe in some sort of pre-deterministic philosophy where everything is set by physics or by the plan of some higher being, in which case you were always meant to be reading this!

Victor Frankl, who was imprisoned during the Second World War in a concentration camp, wrote in his book *Man's Search for Meaning*:

> *When we are no longer able to change a situation, we are challenged to change ourselves. Everything can be taken from a man but one thing: the last of the human freedoms—to choose one's attitude in any given set of circumstances, to choose one's own way. Between stimulus and response there is a space. In that space is our power to choose our response. In our response lies our growth and our freedom.*

He observed that those who survived psychologically were those who had purpose and meaning beyond the terrible situation they were in, and exercised their choice.

So, let's go back to basics and figure out how much time and money you actually have to spare. The chances are it will be a lot more than you realise. If you are in a relationship, like marriage, where you have pooled what you have together and have things that need to be done to support dependants, like children, then you will need to factor that in as appropriate and it may stimulate a conversation with other parties – but try to get a sense of the time and money you have to spare on your own first.

To get a true perspective on how much time and money you really have, you need to go entirely back to basics and completely clear your mind of what is essential and what is a choice (I am afraid the car, television and Netflix account are all gone). Make these assumptions:

➤ you don't want to move to a less nice place to live (but even that is obviously a choice)

➤ you can keep any children you have (but don't have any more)

➤ keep with the same partner (again don't have any more...)

➤ keep any pets you have

➤ keep the same job and schools for your children...

But everything else needs to be challenged.

The Why-Force for Leaders

Let's start with **money**. Essentially, complete your equivalent of the spreadsheet below (this is a good way of doing it as you can add and take things away easily and all the adding up is done for you):

My/our money income	Amount	Times / year	Total
My salary (post tax)	£1,834	12	£22,008
Partner's salary (post tax)	£2,023	12	£24,276
Child allowance	£21	52	£1,092
			£47,376

My/our money expenditure	Amount	Times / year	Total
Mortgage	£565	12	£6,780
Council tax	£246	10	£2,460
My monthly train fare	£212	12	£2,544
My partner's monthly bus fare	£110	12	£1,320
Water	£52	12	£624
Energy	£159	12	£1,908
Phones / Wi-Fi	£60	12	£720
Food	£75	52	£3,900
School bus	£4	180	£720
Child care	£66	52	£3,432
House insurance	£289	1	£289
			£24,697

My/our money remaining per year			**£22,679**

The rules are:

➤ no car (assume you walk or use the cheapest form of public transport everywhere – we will factor in the extra time this may take you in the next exercise)

➤ no television

➤ you are vegetarian, eating only what you absolutely need (doesn't include pain au chocolat)

2: Back to Basics

- no Costa Coffee (tap water only to drink)
- no alcohol
- thermostat set to 15°C
- no non-essential electricity
- no memberships
- one tablet device and a mobile phone with an internet connection good enough to order things on
- but keep paying your utility bills, council bills and insurance (unless you are philosophically opposed to doing so...).

I am not suggesting you live like this, although you may have already identified some unnecessary things that are purely waste and do not really bring you any benefits. It is really about identifying how much choice you have.

John Gummer, when he was minister for transport, said that 'people want good public transport so that everyone else uses it'... well, sorry about the car going, but for this exercise you need to keep assuming you can use public transport if at all possible, and bike and walk everywhere, accepting it takes longer and you might get a bit colder and wetter than you are used to... at least that compensates for the gym membership you just gave up!

Same exercise now for your **time**. The good thing about your 'time income' is that it is exactly the same as that of Elon Musk, Angela Merkel, Richard Branson and Jacinda Ardern... it is the same for everyone and luck has very little to do with what you do with it.

The average adult needs between seven and nine hours' sleep, so please do not skimp on this important factor unless you are very sure you do not need so much. You will also notice that there is a subtotal here to help identify how many hours you would have left living this way on a normal workday. If this number turns negative without the car, then you are allowed to add the car back in for the expenditure too – but again please bear in mind that this exercise is all about recognising how much choice you really have.

The Why-Force for Leaders

My time income	Hours	Times / year	Total
Hours	24	365	**8760**

My time expenditure	Hours	Times / year	Total
Sleep	8	365	2920
Cooking & eating	0.75	365	274
Personal hygiene	0.25	365	91
Washing dishes	0.15	365	55
Walking dog	0.75	365	274
Looking after Mum	1	365	365
Average hours at work	8	228	1824
Walking child to bus	0.6	228	137
Helping with home work	0.75	228	171
Walk to & from station	0.8	228	182
Train to & from work	1.2	228	274
Work day hours taken up	**22**		
Maintaining garden	2	12	24
Cleaning house	1.5	52	78
Washing clothes	0.5	52	26
Shopping	1	52	52
			6746
My time remaining per year			**2014**
Hours/day spare: workday:	**1.8**	average:	**5.5**

That is it, job done. Hopefully you have now identified how much choice you really have and, what is more, you have even more if you factor in where you live, what job you choose to do and whether or not you keep Rover (your dog... I am assuming you have not called your child Rover... if you have, then I'd like to suggest an alternative course of action).

Now we are going to move on to start defining what you, personally, are all about... your Why.

3 The End

I know, it's an odd name for Chapter 3 of a book, but bear with me. In one of the most influential books of the 20th century, *The 7 Habits of Highly Effective People*, Stephen Covey encourages us at the start of his 'Begin with the end in mind' habit to complete an extremely powerful exercise, where he gets you to imagine your funeral and what people say about you. I suspect most people who read the book might not have done so as fully as Covey intended, so in my adaptation of that exercise it is time to put that wrong to right.

You are going to need at least 30 uninterrupted minutes to complete this to a good first level, so switch off the phone, emails and tell everyone to leave you alone...

I want you to shut your eyes for a second and imagine it is your 70th birthday party. If you are already over 70, go for the next significant birthday. The people you love in the world are all there, all of your friends, colleagues from clubs or societies you were part of and also close business contacts. Picture the room. Note how people are dressed. Listen to the atmosphere. Register the body language. Do not move on until you have a clear picture, a clear soundtrack and a clear feeling of the occasion.

A close member of your family – think who that will be, perhaps the one who will put things the best and you were particularly close to – is now walking to the front of the room and picking up the microphone. They now begin to speak... about you, about who you are as a person, what you stand for, perhaps things that you are most proud of or achieved, but above all about your character and how you are with people.

The Why-Force for Leaders

What do you hope they will be saying? Take at least five minutes to draft this first part of your 70th birthday speech. It will of course be positive. But the exercise is about what you hope they will be saying, so that is natural – do not hold back trying to be modest.

It's now the turn of one of your closest friends. Again, pause and think who that will be and imagine them making their way to the front of the room and picking up the microphone. Take at least five minutes to write down what you hope they will say about how you are among your friends, your character, your talents you bring to those friendship groups and what you are like as a friend. This forms the second part of your 70th birthday speech.

Next up is someone from your community, perhaps a club or society or charity or church that you have a lot to do with. Who would be the best person to say a few words? Imagine they are walking to the front, past your other friends and family, and they begin to speak. What do you hope they will be saying about your character, your achievements and your contribution to the communities that you are part of? Take five minutes to note down a first draft of that too.

Finally, and not surprisingly for a leader, imagine someone from perhaps the business that you had or still have most to do with or achieved the most with, is making that same journey to the front of the room. Who do you hope that will be? Take another five minutes to note down what you hope they will be saying about your achievements in the business world and how you conducted yourself.

Over the next week or so – and please do not rush this – I want you to imagine that all four speeches are coming together to be delivered by the person you would most like to be giving one overall speech on your 70th birthday. Maybe add some of your personal history, place of birth, formative years, etc. to the start of that speech. It might help you pick up some things that have already happened that you have missed, as perhaps you were focused on achievements that are yet to happen in the initial exercise. Save this file and make a diary note to keep looking at it every three months or so. It is a fantastic starting point for figuring out what is of most importance to you... and very much some (not quite) end-in-mind thinking.

This is a hugely rich and important text for you, but it is hard to look at it frequently enough, so I'd like you now to begin the process of forming this into a one-pager of your values and purpose (your Why) that you can reference during your two to five minutes' thinking time each day. I suggest you note down on it both the daily action you will take towards your goals and your daily Beacon (although you may already have a better system working for you to record those).

Start the process by pulling out all the values that are important to you from your 70th birthday speech. They could be things like fun, creativity, people, hard work, fairness, etc. In the first few weeks of developing this – yes, I'm afraid this is not an exercise you can complete in five minutes – just start noting them all down as you'll see on the 'early days' example below. You do not have to use this template; you could choose to use the page of a book or write them on your computer or an app on a tablet/phone... just make sure it achieves the same purpose of noting them down and keeping on looking at them and refining them.

At the same time, start to form a picture of your purpose and goals, your personal vision. This combination of your values and your vision will form a large part of your Personal Why.

The best way that I have found is forming a series of overlapping circles, which is a concept that I have adapted over the years since reading the excellent book *No Regrets on Sunday* by Dr Peter Hawkins. First I want you to think about the three to six most important areas of your life... I am talking about general areas that come out time and again in your 70th birthday speech. For instance, it could be family, career, charity work, friends, hobbies or health. As with the 'early days' example below, draw them as a series of overlapping circles. The size of the circles represents how important they are to you and the overlaps, which you will note are probably quite large, represent the crossovers between these two or three areas – for instance, you might play tennis, a *hobby*, with a *friend* and it is also good for your *health*.

Now start to populate the areas inside the circles and particularly inside the Venn diagram-type overlaps with statements of how you would like things to be in three years' time (you can add some longer-term elements to this personal vision too). VERY IMPORTANTLY, start the process by adding the elements of your life that are currently in place and are exactly as you wish them to be or very close to being so. It is so important to recognise the richness that already exists in our lives, as starting with a blank canvas can actually be demotivating.

As an aside on the power of shrinking down the size of the change we need to make, in their book *Switch* Chip and Dan Heath reference the story of a car wash in the US which used to have a system where you got given a card and if you collected five stamps you got a free car wash (a bit like the McDonald's bean stickers for coffee). They then changed the system so you had to get eight stamps, but the card you were given had the first three already stamped (so you still in effect needed five to get a free car wash). The uptake went up significantly, because people were no longer starting from scratch. No logic there, just an observation on human motivation, so it is really important to recognise all the great things in your life that you already have in place. For a lot of people, this is also more than they realise when they stop and think about it.

It is important that you put down a **SMART** version of your personal vision:

➤ 'S' stands for **Specific** – without making it very long, describe what exactly you want in a word, symbol or picture... it just has to make sense to you.

➤ 'M' stands for **Measurable** – give it a number, a frequency, even a subjective 9 out of 10 rating (e.g. when it comes to things like how confident or fulfilled you or others feel, if that is part of your vision).

➤ 'A' stands for **Attainable** – do not just put down pipe dreams that you know you will never achieve.

➤ 'R' stands for **Relevant** – simply do not put down things that you do not care about (if you did not mention them as part of your 70th birthday speech, question if you do really care about that element of your vision enough to want to make it happen).

➤ 'T' stands for **Time-bound** – is there a particular date by which you want to achieve this or are you already doing so and want to maintain it? You may also want to reference interim goals... stepping stones along the way that again help to shrink the change somewhat and not make it too daunting.

Really enjoy spending some quality time pulling this together and do not worry if it looks like a bit of mess to start with. Over the coming weeks, it will start to simplify as you find better ways to express this. Again, as with values, you might not want to use the template and instead write it down in a notebook (I would recommend one page per significant area of your life) or put it down electronically.

Once you have completed the first version, I would recommend re-filling in the template one more time and seeing if you can pull things together and simplify it so you end up with something a bit like the 'early days' example below.

Then, pick some specific times (I recommend making notes in your diary) to redo your whole Personal Why in a week's time, two weeks later than that and then a month after that. By then it should have come together and you will have noticed what you are doing something about and what you are not doing anything about (probably the things you need to remove as you do not actually care about them enough). This will happen naturally by focusing on it and you will rapidly develop a version of your Personal Why that looks like the 'steady state' example below the 'early days' example (overleaf):

The Why-Force for Leaders

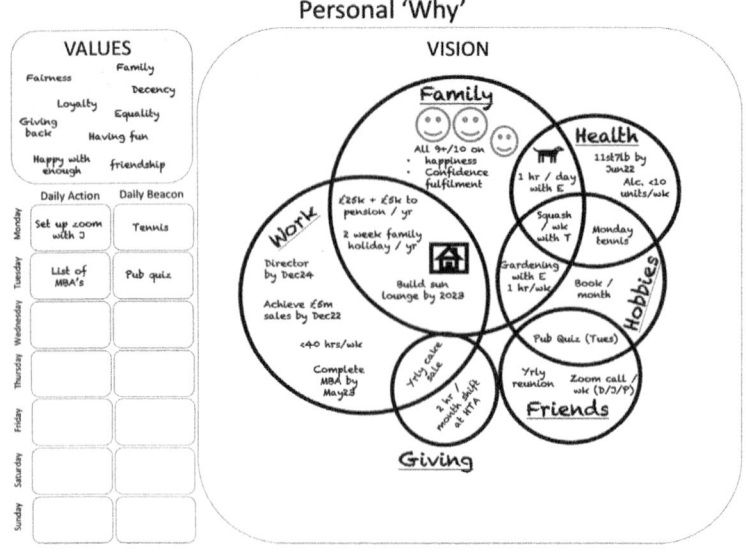

'Early days' example of Personal Why

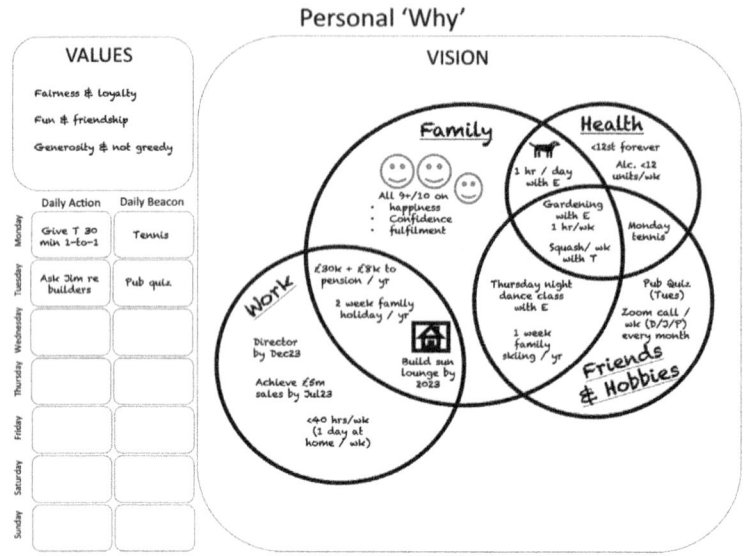

'Steady state' example of Personal Why

3: The End

It is important to look at your Personal Why regularly, so you will probably have picked up by now that your two to five minutes' thinking time that you have established as a habit since Chapter 1 is your ideal time to do so. The one daily action and the daily Beacon on the template, if you are using it, are the places to add those in. Take a photocopy each time you complete a new version of your Personal Why (I have mine done electronically) and use it as the starting template for each week. You will start to notice some rapid progress – not luck! – towards the areas of your Personal Why that you actually care most about. Do not be afraid to delete the other stuff that you are not doing anything about... these were probably in the 'shoulds' or 'worthy goals' categories.

4　Less Is More

There's the classic Tommy Cooper joke about the man who goes to the doctor and says, raising his arm, 'Doctor, it hurts every time I do this.' The doctor replies, 'Well, don't do it then.' Trivial though it sounds, if you have not got much time, do less. Or rather, make sure you spend more time this week than you did last week on areas of your life that are important to you – 'important' defined as aligned to your Personal Why.

There are two approaches to this:

1 Focus on doing more of the 'important'.
2 Spend less time on what is less 'important' or of no importance.

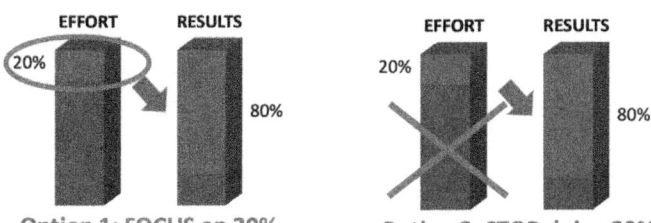

Option 1: FOCUS on 20%   Option 2: STOP doing 80%

Now, you may think they are one and the same, or be slightly irritated by how obvious this sounds. But do bear with me.

ALERT! Be extremely careful not to view your time as a to-do list of tasks. One of the most important uses of your time is listening to others. This will not appear on such a list. And although you can be proactive adding things like 'call Mum', for the people around us it will not work to say 'this is the time I have allocated in my busy schedule to listen to you'!

So, keep on picking one action per day that takes you one step towards your Personal Why. Anchor it into your diary or do it first thing. Make it as powerful as it can be, while making sure it still gets done. You will have noticed that, even if you take quite a bit of time, the things you had to do that day also got done. If you take 365 actions towards your Personal Why, that is going to represent a huge amount of progress in a year. And keep putting a Beacon in your diary every day. It is important to sustain your energy.

Most people who adopt this approach stop here and do enjoy the benefits of doing so. But they remain very busy doing stuff that is actually not that important to their Personal Why. Some of the less important stuff stops, but nowhere near enough. Warren Buffett and Steve Jobs are both well known for what they have achieved. However, they would both reference their ability to say 'no' as a key ingredient to staying focused.

Jony Ive, or Sir Jonathan Ive to you and me, who used to have the wonderful title of Head of Customer Experience at Apple (all companies should have one) tells the story that Steve Jobs was always coming up to him and saying 'What have you said "no" to today?' After a while, he developed a bank of made-up things to reply with! Admittedly, this sounds like it was not therefore working, but actually Jobs was repetitively asking the same important question... a wonderfully effective way to help people form a habit (even if they seemed to be giving him the brush-off). Warren Buffett is the same. He has always focused on eliminating the 80 per cent from the stuff below rather than just focusing on the 20 per cent.

So, how to say 'no' more... There are essentially three strategies:

1. Be more aware of what is important to you... you are essentially already doing this by looking at your Personal Why every day. You will therefore naturally start to reject things that do not align with your vision or values and accept more of those that are.
2. Look at everything you have to do, rank them in terms of importance from 1 to 10 and not do those of that rank

below a 5 that you can possibly get away with not doing. If you already write everything down in a system, go ahead and do that now. If you do not, start a system to do so now... it can only be of benefit. And then, do that exercise.

3. Write a 'not-to-do' list. Buffett calls this his 'avoid-at-any-cost list'. Go ahead and start that now. If you have a to-do list system, just add this now. If not, start it on paper or electronically. This should include anything that crept on to your to-do list that should not have got there, anything in the past that you regret saying 'yes' to and anything you can anticipate you will be asked to do or take part in in the future that you need to be saying 'no' to. Go ahead! Start making that list.

Now, you do need to cover off communicating your decisions. 'Sorry mate, I decided when reading this book last night that I did not want to play tennis any more' will not go down well with the person on the phone who has spent the last 10 minutes warming up their serve.

And some things you have decided not to do are going to take a while to extricate yourself from. Say you are on a committee or doing a voluntary role for an organisation that you care about; leaving today is not going to be aligned to your values... probably. So, simply start putting those decisions in motion. Often it is going to need a fairly direct, but awkward conversation, but just resolve to do so as soon as possible. You will feel so much better when you do. Do not make the mistake of putting it off as this will sap your energy.

Finally, you need to be armed and ready to say 'no' nicely. I'm not talking about cold callers, who you can choose to either just hang up on or spend two or three minutes politely saying goodbye (I may have inadvertently leaked what I do...). I'm talking about people you care about who have asked you to do something. There's a three-step process that I would recommend trying at least twice in the next week:

The Why-Force for Leaders

1. Say 'yes'... well, actually say 'Yes, I understand why you have asked me to do that...' Acknowledge that their request is not based on fresh lunacy. No one particularly likes to hear the word 'no' at the start of a reply. So, develop your version of the 'Yes, ...' statement – one that you feel comfortable using.

2. Then, state what you are focused on. You should now be clearer on your priorities, your Personal Why, so this should be a lot easier to articulate now. How many times have you said 'yes' and then thought 'I wish that I'd mentioned how busy I am on this other thing'?

3. Finally, the really important thing to keep is rapport. Suggest an alternative... 'What if I sent across the information I have on that?' or any other credible suggestion. It does not have to be one they take up. Just try to be genuinely helpful without saying 'yes'.

That's it... keep focusing on what is important to you. Remember, things like listening to people you love are so important and not on any to-do list, and it is rarely something you can precisely time – but you can be proactive in some ways, like going on a walk.

And say 'no' nicely at least twice in the next week. Next up we will be considering whether you are in the right teams or environments that are going to allow you to keep to your values, achieve your vision and acquire new skills and habits. There might be a few more tweaks to make there...

5 New Skills

When socialising venues got shut down in the coronavirus pandemic, a group of my friends decided, as many others did, that the only option was to take our pub group online to keep us all relatively sane (or at least to maintain the level of sanity we were at). A format naturally emerged that we all enjoyed... chat, quiz, pool (don't ask) and music (one of my friends plays the guitar). So, a couple of weeks in, I decided to have a go myself on the guitar. My wife is a fantastic musician, so she lent me one of her guitars and showed me a few simple chords and off I went learning a new song on the guitar and singing along to it every week.

A few weeks later, my wife and daughter were sitting together in a room nearby when I was 'performing' my latest song. Hearing me playing and singing the song, shall we say less than perfectly, my daughter turned to my wife and grimaced. 'Don't worry, he'll still get clapped,' was my wife's response. And... as every week previously, I did! Not only did I get clapped, but I got genuinely (I think) thanked and encouraged.

The point of this story is that if part of your personal vision is to develop new skills or new habits, you need to do it in the right environment and, often, with the right team of people. In fact, in order to achieve your Personal Why, you also need to be in the right teams. Those teams must give you the support you need and should not clash with your personal values.

Start by recognising which new skills you need to acquire in order to achieve your Personal Why. List them all down now (ignore the 'actions/notes' side of the example overleaf for now). For instance, you might have:

Skills	Actions / notes
Learn to create videos	Need lessons
Take badminton to 2nd team level	Get mentor
Become a chartered marketeer	On course
Get recommendations	Set up team
Learn patio maintenance	Ask Bob for advice
Learn to grow veg	Form group

Ignore the ones you are going to acquire on your own… although keep an eye on yourself actually getting on with them. You might need an accountability team or the help of a mentor!

If you think about my guitar story, you need the right conditions in place to acquire a new skill:

- ➤ burning desire
- ➤ regular commitment
- ➤ a mentor
- ➤ a role model
- ➤ cheerleaders
- ➤ a small-steps plan
- ➤ a fixed date to perform.

Mohammad Ali famously said, 'I hated every minute of training, but I said, "Don't quit. Suffer now and live the rest of your life as a champion."' With some skills, which you want to acquire and it's not going to be fun doing so, you need to project yourself into thinking about the future state you have a burning desire to reach. Although be careful to only have a maximum of one of these types of skill acquisition in your life. As someone once said, 'self-restraint is a finite resource'.

So, in my case:

- I love the thought of playing the guitar and singing... more so than my audiences!
- I met up with a group of friends every week and they were going to ask me to play something.
- My wife mentored me and I had a book.
- One of my friends inspired me with his guitar playing, so acted as a role model.
- I still got clapped by my friends (cheerleaders).
- I set a list of six sing-a-long sounds I wanted to learn which I played to a basic level and then improved.
- When lockdown ended, I was able to play all six around the firepit with my friends singing along.

If you are very good at researching things or figuring things out for yourself, then perhaps you can acquire new skills on your own, but I would reframe how you look at things to include the team (or person) whose book you read or whose demonstration videos you watch as part of your team. There are very few instances when acquiring a new skill with absolutely no support really works.

With the above in mind, to the right of your list of skills, it's time to complete the actions you need to take or the notes on what you already have in place, as in my example above. With all those things in place, it should feel harder *not* to acquire the new skill than to do so!

Now to turn to **habits**. Some of your Personal Why will involve getting rid of some bad habits or acquiring some new, better ones. It is actually often easier to frame it as acquiring a new one, so long as this is what you are genuinely doing. Take, say, giving up smoking. Do not be tempted to try and frame this 'breathing more fresh air'... You won't fool yourself.

List the habits you are looking to form or give up, e.g.:

➤ Eat a better, balanced, sensible amount of food and avoid eating late at night.

➤ Only drink alcohol when with friends and avoid ever having a hangover.

Again, referencing Mohammad Ali, you probably do need to project your thinking more into the future, particularly if you really enjoy cheese and red wine! This example might be a little close to home. The problem is that a lot of the benefits you will gain are probably a way off. For instance, if you knew that by drinking a glass of wine you would die the next day, you would not drink it. If, as is the reality, you will probably get some pretty unpleasant health conditions at some point in the future unless you moderate your behaviour, you might very well take your chances.

There's really no easy solution here unless you ask someone to hypnotise you. You simply have to believe so much in the long-term benefits that a switch goes off in your mind that says you are now going to always live like that with the new positive habits or without the bad ones. When you have this mindset, you will achieve it. When you don't, you will probably yoyo through dry January fads and your New Year's resolutions will last less time than your hangover. Make up your mind and then do it forever, not for a few weeks. You might want to think about joining a support team too, if appropriate. Good luck!

Now take a moment to note down the other personal teams you are in. A team can be anything from you plus one other to a whole sports team or a large organisational team. So, any family you are with is a team. If you play tennis with someone every week, that is a team. If you are part of a social group, that is a team. Your work is undoubtedly carried out as part of a team. But if you do all your house/garden maintenance on your own that is just you. Or, if you play the piano just for enjoyment on your own that is not a team either. Here's an example list of teams you might be in:

As a Team	Notes
Living as family	In place
Business goals	Need to find a mentor
Maintaining the house	Painter, joiner and electrician missing
Pub group	In place
Couple friendship groups	Need one more regular social
Financial planning	In place
School friends group	Not set up
Overseas friend	Not set up

Simply make some notes to the side of each team you are in about what needs setting up or whether things are already in place. Recognising these gaps and then doing something about them is as simple as it needs to be.

The only other factor to consider is **values**. Hopefully your values are coming together into a set of three meaningful ones. You just need to consider whether any of your teams go against your personal values or maybe even mean you cannot achieve your personal vision if you are in them. You may conclude you need to leave a particular team or that is just a misalignment of values that you have to tolerate because of a lack of choice... although we normally have more choice than we initially perceive.

That's us done on the personal front. It is vitally important that you maintain all of what we have covered so far, so that you can bring the energy and focus to your leadership role that your team deserves. Now, we'll take a look at those leadership skills.

6 The Infinite Cycle

We now turn our attention to the team that you lead. It might be that you lead the whole organisation or a large or small team within it. It does not matter.

Ultimately, where you need to get to is a point where you are positively influencing the Infinite Cycle shown below:

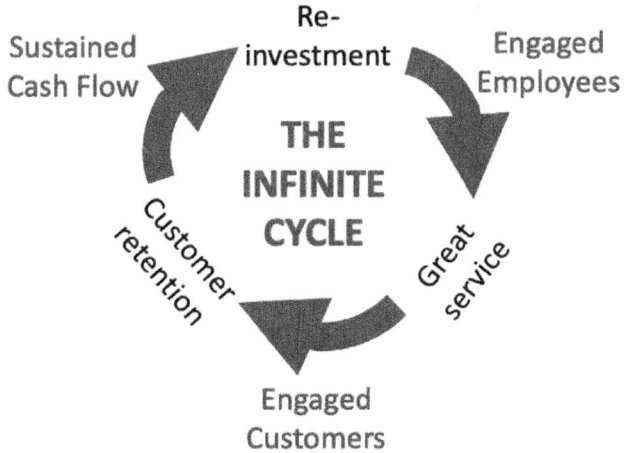

We will keep coming back to this, so it is worth taking a few moments to start looking at it.

By definition, you have employees in your team (if you don't then you might want to reconsider whether you are a leader!). If they are truly engaged, they will provide a great service to your customers. Your customers could be external (and definitely will be if you are in charge of the whole organisation) or they could be internal if you, say, look after the IT infrastructure or finance function or part of an operation, etc. This will satisfy your customers, who will retain you. If you are not providing a good internal service, your internal customers will quite rightly try and exit you. Customer retention will lead to sustained cash flow if it is the whole business (cash flow just meaning you make positive cash). If it is an internal team, your equivalent of cash flow might be something like computer uptime. Generating this will lead to reinvestment in your team. This will further engage your employees, and on we go.

You must firstly dispel all doubts that you might not be 100% responsible for your team's Infinite Cycle... good or bad. If you feel you are not, have an open and honest conversation with your line manager or maybe the business owners, and then leave if you can't sort this out. What is the point in being a leader if you are not responsible for leading?

Still got a job? Good! You must insist on and enjoy having the responsibility. Never as leaders can we blame others. Take ownership and thrive on it!

The second thing is best described by a simple analogy. You are not going to start cutting the lawn while your house is burning down... unless you are Emperor Nero (playing the fiddle while Rome burns). Equally, you are not going to start figuring out how to improve your team if your team is catastrophically failing to do what it needs to do.

We are all naturally very energised in a crisis. So, if there is a fire, concentrate on helping your team put it out first, before reading on. It would be like saying to your partner 'Let's sit down and improve how we communicate as a couple' while your children had gone missing. Your team will rightly not be receptive to this and will lose confidence in you.

Now, you might slip into the trap of thinking there is always a crisis. This is actually quite a dangerous mindset or situation for a leader and a team. If it is real, it is often generated by doing too many unprofitable things for too many clients or you may need more resources (temporarily or permanently). But, more often than not, it is a mindset and it is important to get things in perspective.

6: The Infinite Cycle

Completing the next exercise will help you in both situations. As with the exercise on personal time and money, it is all about seeing you have a level of choice available.

Firstly, for your team, who is your customer? As discussed above, this could be internal or external. It is going to be helpful in future chapters to start to get a picture of who this ideal customer is for your team.

Secondly, what do you physically do for them? Don't worry for now about the Why of this – we'll come to that later. Just think about the physical outputs you produce for them. This will be the product or service your team provides. It could be, say, a medical device or internally it could be financial data or it could be IT fixes.

Now imagine your team is a small independent business which has customers who are so happy that you never have review meetings with them and you have a ready supply of recommendations from customers, so you do not need to market your product or service. You have no internal meetings, and everything you need to do from a compliance or regulatory point of view is taken care of. In short, all you and your team have to do is produce your product or service.

The only thing you have to cover every month is the fixed cost of your team existing: salaries (include everyone in your team's monthly wages); offices/production space/rates (if you need them); and other unavoidable non-product or service-specific expenses (these should be quite low). If you are the leader of a whole organisation, this is just your average monthly fixed costs. What is that figure?

The question is: how much do you have to deliver for your ideal customers in order to cover the largely fixed cost of your team existing? You will need to have a think about the mix of products or services that you produce. You will have to factor in the additional cost of delivering each of these units of product or service (parts or external services bought in, delivery, certification, etc.). If you provide a product or service to an internal customer, you will need to do some research to determine what your internal customer would have to pay for that product or service if they bought it in externally.

The Why-Force for Leaders

This shows you how much of your core value-adding activity as a team you need to do in order not to be a financial burden to your business. You might also want to factor in owner or company board expectations, but essentially it is healthy to have a picture, as a team, of what you need to do to keep your head above water.

Of course, we never want to let our customers down and we are usually trying to grow our team's customer base, but once again it is important to connect with the choices you are making.

Perhaps when you look at this, you might decide to cut down on some less profitable activities. You might even decide not to serve certain customers. In the long term, you want to focus just on your core key customers and your team's Why... the change you make in the world. So, this could be the start of that journey.

The key for now is to get things in perspective, so you know what you need to do and what you are choosing to do... as with your personal time, you probably have more choice as a team than you realise.

The choice that I would encourage you to make is to only do things that positively influence the Infinite Cycle. Measure employee engagement and customer satisfaction and have two or three key measures relating to cash flow or the equivalent.

7 Rock Time

There's a well-used analogy referencing a science lesson experiment about how to fit rocks, gravel and sand into a jar. If you put the gravel or sand in first, it doesn't work. The only way to make it work is to put the rocks in first, then the gravel and then the sand.

In the analogy, the Rocks are your really important tasks as a leader which, if you get them done, will lead to the long-term success of your team. They are a bit like the daily actions you take towards your personal vision. The fact they are big rocks does not mean they are going to take a lot of time. In fact, often the reverse. The gravel represents your value-adding tasks, the things that contribute fairly directly to the delivery of your product or service. The sand represents everything else.

What are the Rocks for you?

These tend to be the type of actions that are not particularly urgent, but do have a huge impact on the long-term success of your team. They might take you slightly outside your comfort zone. They might take a bit of thinking and planning time. They are the activities that accelerate the Infinite Cycle we looked at in Chapter 6.

Start making a list of them on a sheet of paper. Here are some thoughts to get you started:

- time with your core customers understanding their present and future needs, and gathering feedback on how you as a team are doing
- taking time to walk around, meet people and understand better the function of your team

- doing research or talking to people or attending conferences on what the future of your industry might look like
- doing research into developing technologies that might replace what you do
- keeping up regular, state-of-the-nation type communications with your whole team during which they can ask questions and bring up any concerns
- sitting down and developing a clear, one-page plan (more on that later)
- spending one-to-one time with a member of your team, helping them develop and coaching them on a plan for their role and personal development
- just thinking (alone or as a team)
- engaging in a project, such as marketing or product development, to transform the long-term success of your team
- spending time doing team bonding.

What else? Note that all of the above could be put off until tomorrow, next week, indefinitely, except, if it is, it risks the long-term success of your team.

So, draw a large jar like the one opposite on a sheet of paper. The jar represents how much time you choose to dedicate to your role. Now, putting aside the shape of the rocks (to avoid your diagram getting really complicated), make an estimate of how much time you spend on Rocks, how much on gravel and how much on sand.

Now make a list of which Rocks you need to find time for and put into your diary first. And what gravel and sand should you stop doing? If there is anything you can eliminate that is not a Rock and will have no impact on your team's long-term success, just stop doing it now (remember the Tommy Cooper joke in Chapter 4).

7: Rock Time

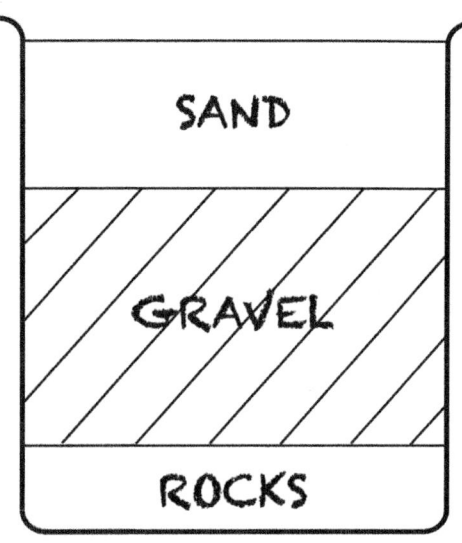

Now, it is true that if you do the Rocks first, everything else still tends to happen. However, sometimes there is a bit too much gravel and sand, so we need to develop this a bit further. Also, there is a possibility that some of your Rocks are the wrong ones! DO NOT use this as a reason not to do the Rocks first. Just resolve to be clearer on why your Rocks are important and to do something about the excess gravel and sand. This excess is probably stopping you doing really important activities such as listening to and supporting people.

So, let's look at how you use your time. Re-create the Desire–Ability matrix overleaf. The horizontal axis represents how much you like doing a particular task and the vertical axis represents how good you think you are at doing the same task. Ignore the angled line for now; we will come to that in a bit.

Think of all the things you do during the hours you choose to work in an average week and add them to the matrix with an estimate of how many hours you spend on that task in an average week (ignore the asterisks for now). It is best to complete this exercise over a few days as it is hard to think of everything you do at once… there is always something that occurs to you the next day.

The Why-Force for Leaders

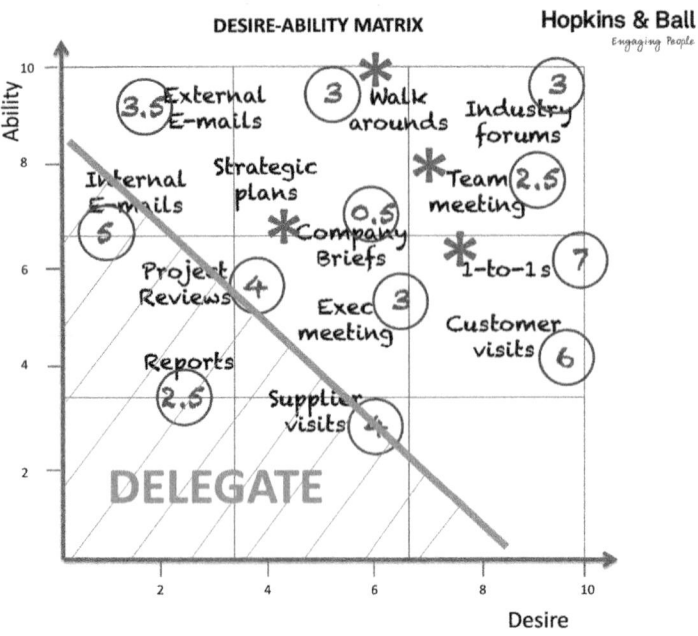

All done? Great. Now put an asterisk beside any of the activities that are to do with managing people (one-to-ones, weekly meetings, coaching, development and support, dealing with people issues, etc.). If all those are in the low desire end of the chart, you probably should not consider furthering your career as a leader... sorry! I suggest looking for more of a technical lead/director-type role.

Now ask yourself, how many hours a week would you like to be working? Say you go for 40 hours. I suggest taking 80 per cent of that figure (so 32 hours) and drawing an angled line to give activities worth 32 hours to the top and right of that. Everything to the bottom and left of that line is tasks that you need to consider delegating if at all possible. The reason for the 80 per cent is that you need to free up some time for leadership activities that you have not as yet decided to do.

In general, people and leaders do not always delegate as much as they should. Here is a list of some typical reasons people give:

- Being good at these activities got me promoted in the first place.
- I have no one to delegate to.
- It takes too much time for me to train someone.
- I find that it's faster and easier to do it myself.
- I wouldn't ask anyone to do anything I wouldn't do myself.
- No one can do it as well as me.
- It's too complicated to explain it to them.
- I spend too much time fixing their mistakes.

All of the above will limit you as a leader. So, if they really are true, you need to solve them. Often, they are not true… be really honest with yourself!

Take a few moments to make a list and commit to delegating the tasks that you need to. And then take a small step towards doing so. Something like drafting an email to set up a meeting will do. Commit to these actions – even if it causes some short-term pain and extra effort. Most leaders need to delegate more so they can free up their time to properly lead and drive forward the Infinite Cycle.

8 Team Why

There are a number of organisations that, when you stop and think about it, should not really exist. Take Tesla. I refer to its place in the electric vehicles market. Over the previous 50 years, some powerful car manufacturers had more opportunity than Tesla has ever had to do what Tesla has done. The same with Netflix. Likewise, in the UK, Ocado with online deliveries. Incumbents in those markets had the money and resources to have done what all those companies did better and earlier. But they didn't. Because they were too focused on their existing products or services rather than the change they could make in the world.

If we fast forward another 50 years, the chances are that the products and services that you provide will not exist either. The change you make for your customers will probably still be a need... although not always!

In Chapter 6, you considered (you may have already clearly known) who the ideal customer of the team you lead is, whether they are internal or external and receiving a product or service from your team.

You can do the following exercise on your own first if you like, but the exponential benefit comes from doing it with your team with an open mind. So do not get too fixed to your ideas.

Imagine the same ideal customer 50 years from now. Nearly everything will change in the next 50 years. Now, some bad news to absorb: imagine the current product or service you offer was made illegal around 25 years beforehand by a unilateral agreement across all governments of the world.

The good news is that a Silicon Valley entrepreneur (perhaps one of Elon Musk's grandchildren) has invented a magic wand. It sounds trivial, but bear with me!

By waving that wand your ideal customer is able to have exactly whatever your product or service does for them. If you sell drills, they can wave the wand and have the right-sized holes where they want them. If you are a doctor, their medical condition disappears. If you do internal finances, they now have the financial information in front of them. Not exactly an ideal customer any more.

As I mentioned, it is fine to have a go at this on your own to get used to the exercise, but set up a meeting now to gather your team together. Then brief them about your products and services no longer existing and the magic wand being invented, and then break out into groups of three to six for brainstorms on what that wave of the magic wand does.

That wave of the wand is the change your team makes in the world. It sums up why the world is a better place for your team existing. Doing this exercise may also start to prompt some ideas of how your product or service might change in the future. This is the key role of 'the seer'... understanding new technology and options that might develop or replace what you do is a key role in the organisation.

Then, and it may take several weeks, get your team together several times over the coming weeks and months to craft your all-important Why-Statement (as we'll refer to going forward). Go ahead and schedule that first meeting now.

In his fantastic book *The Infinite Game*, Simon Sinek suggests that your purpose, i.e. your team Why should be:

➤ something affirmative and optimistic

➤ inclusive and open to all those who would like to contribute

➤ service orientated – primarily for the benefit of others

➤ resilient – able to endure political, technological and cultural change

➤ idealistic – big, bold and ultimately unachievable.

It also needs to be something that makes sense to and inspires your people, your customers, your suppliers and the wider world.

And as with values, which we will come on to in the next chapter, it needs to work internally and externally. It needs to make customers and suppliers want to do business with you. It needs to make your team want to be part of it. It needs to make talented, like-minded individuals want to join you.

Unfortunately, like most good things, it does not come to you and your team overnight. One of my favourite Why-Statements is from Kimpton Energy Solutions, who essentially plumb and wire services in to buildings, maintain them and create acoustic solutions. Their customers are all over the UK and, like a lot of companies, their purpose and values were pretty well understood internally without being formalised. But formalising is helping to get everyone aligned.

Kimpton's Why-Statement is:

'Creating the sustainable building environments of tomorrow.'

It seems simple. And, like a lot of simple things, it took over three years to come up with. In fact, at Hopkins & Ball, the organisation my wife and I run, we took even longer to come up with:

'Helping organisations create engaging, sustainable jobs.'

You will know when you get there. Do not rush it. At the time of writing this book there are a number of organisations that we have worked with for over two years who are still getting there. If you are a team within an organisation, you need to have a Why-Statement that acknowledges your part in the organisation's overall purpose.

So, if your organisation says 'Saves lives' like Howorth Air Technology (another fantastic organisation that we work with), but you look after the financials, then your purpose needs to acknowledge that your team:

'Provides all the financial information for timely decisions…

… so that we as an organisation can…

… save lives.'

The Why-Force for Leaders

Jim Liptrot, managing director of Howorth Air Technology, shared a powerful story with me about how this Why-Statement is so important. They had had to open up new premises to service an order for some equipment to support a new type of cancer treatment. The contractual negotiations had been dragging on about the lease. Then, in a group call with all parties, everyone was asked if they had anything more to add. Jim raised his hand and said that, although he understood each party had to protect their interests, the effect of this delay was costing lives as cancer treatment was delayed. Nothing aggressive... just the facts and the purpose of Howorth. By the next Monday, they had the keys.

Again, another fantastic organisation that we work with, Compass Minerals – which essentially mines salt to put on the roads – now recognises that its core purpose is to 'Keep Britain moving'. Interestingly, Gordon Dunn and the team at the Winsford mine also have a second business called DeepStore which stores documents and assets in the fantastic natural conditions created by a salt mine. So, they have another Why-Statement for that business, which is 'Keeping valued items secure and accessible'. In each business, the staff recognise that their work is far more important than just digging stuff up and storing stuff.

So, you've started the process of understanding why your team exists and what good it does in the world. A bit like your personal vision, but shorter. It seems counterintuitive that a single person's reason to exist is longer than an organisation's, but in some ways that is the art of leadership... to distil things down to the simplest form (whereas individuals are more complex). Do not rush this. It is natural that it takes some time.

The US President during the First World War, Woodrow Wilson, was asked how long he normally spent preparing to talk. 'That depends on the length of the speech,' he replied. 'If it is a ten-minute speech it takes me all of two weeks to prepare it; if it is a half-hour speech it takes me a week; if I can talk as long as I want to it requires no preparation at all. I am ready now.'

You need to start with the 'ready now' version and then form the 'two weeks to prepare' version over a number of weeks or months.

9 Team Values

The other half of your Personal Why was your values. Hopefully you've distilled those down to three and are looking at them regularly. For an organisation, these values are in some ways more important than the Why-Statement. This is because it is easier for an individual to connect with their own values than for a whole group of people to agree to all behave in ways aligned to a common set of values. It's actually quite important that these are consistent across a whole organisation, so if you run a team and the values are defined for the whole organisation, you may not be able to change them. I would still recommend doing the following exercise though... It might come in useful when you go on to be the leader of the whole organisation!

Again, I would recommend gathering your team together to complete this exercise. Why would you not want to get their input? It's a further opportunity to get buy-in and engagement. You will also get better ideas.

Imagine a date in the future when your organisation has reached a significant milestone. It needs to be at least 20 years out. By then, you may well be providing your product and service in a completely different way, but still delivering your Why-Statement. The milestone could be a 75th anniversary of the founding of the business, it could be reaching a particular size or it could be picking up an industry award. Pick the event now.

Now, there are going to be four speeches (sounds familiar?). They might all reference achievements too, but the majority of the speeches will be focused on what it was like to work in or with your team. As a team, get a clear picture of these four people and then brainstorm, just in note form, what they will say in their speech. I would recommend everyone making their own notes on the four speeches first and then consolidating thoughts on a whiteboard and further brainstorming, one speech at a time.

The four people who are going to deliver these speeches are:

1. An employee who will have worked there for two years at the time of this milestone (so by definition, you have not met this person yet).

2. An employee who will have worked there for 15 years at the time of this milestone and has progressed to executive level (again, you've not met them yet).

3. One of your ideal customers (maybe take some time to define who this is).

4. One of the suppliers that you have a long-term partnership with (again, take some time to define who this is).

From this exercise, pull out a list of all the values and behaviours that have been referenced. Try and cluster them together as much as possible. You might start with, say, 20 to 30 values and behaviours and manage to cluster them down to around 10 to 12. Once you've done so, give everyone five votes to mark against each of these consolidated values. This helps pick out the ones that are most important.

Ultimately, you need to get to three values. In organisations with more than three values, often the executive team cannot remember them and you find that, without considerable effort, only about one in ten people can easily remember them. In other words, they cannot be referenced as people make day-to-day decisions.

It is sometimes hard to consolidate this list down to three, so you may want to set three core values and use the other values and behaviours referenced as part of the explanation of what the three core values mean. For instance, at Hopkins & Ball our values are:

9: Team Values

- **Walk the talk** (Keep It Simple, Practise the 7 Factors Model, Measure & Learn)
- **Customer fan base** (Make a Positive Difference, Feel the Quality, Cause Referrals)
- **Appreciate people** (See the Best in Humankind, Make It Fun, Growth Makes Us Thrive)

But in reality we just reference our core values (those in bold above).

Howorth Air Technology has ICE:

- **Integrity**
- **Collaboration**
- **Excellence.**

Kimpton Energy Solutions has FIT:

- **Focus on customers**
- **Integrity in everything**
- **Teamwork wins.**

The Contact Company has TCC:

- **Trust**
- **Courtesy**
- **Communication.**

Active Business Communications has:

- **We take responsibility**
- **We manage change**
- **We work together.**

Always three! Easy to remember *and*, most importantly, like your Why-Statement, something you would be equally happy to share internally and externally. In fact, you hope your customers, suppliers and employees love them and take pride in working with you because you have them. They actually become a powerful marketing tool as a side effect.

Again, do not rush this. It may take several months to develop these. But start now!

It is important to note that these values (or behaviours) can very easily become what I call 'industrial wallpaper'. Just print them up, put them on every wall and people will follow them. Wrong! You need to live and breathe them. You need to hire and fire based on them (more of that in Chapter 10).

So, regardless of how your organisation rewards people, you, as the leader of your team, need to start focusing people on these values. If you have a system for capturing stories of them being lived by, make sure you are using it. If not, do the following to get things started (you can make it more sophisticated later on). Simply...

1. Create a new email folder call 'Living by our values'.
2. Tell your team you are going to capture these stories (and why) and to email them to you as they happen.
3. Add these emails (including ones you've written yourself to this folder).
4. For the first few weeks, send a reminder about emailing these stories on a Thursday.
5. On a Friday, summarise your top five examples in an email to your whole team.
6. Ask them to email you back their votes for the best one.
7. Give the winner a small reward (say a £20 voucher) before they go home.

9: TEAM VALUES

Later on, you can make this more of a system (capturing the stories better, making voting anonymous, etc.), but the above can work forever too and eliminates inertia. Do not worry about starting this before you get to three values. Just use the ones that have been suggested (even if there's a list of 15 to start with). Go ahead! Start living as a team by your values.

10 Right People

Naval Ravikant, co-founder of AngelList, once said, 'If you can't see yourself working with someone for life, don't work with them for a day.'

Yet time and again, leaders tolerate what I call cultural killers. These are the people who do not fit with your team's values or purpose. They may even have some very key skills. But when they leave, the whole organisation heaves a collective sigh of relief and wonders why they did not leave earlier.

Now, do not misunderstand this. Give anyone a chance to change. But when you reach the point of knowing that someone will never be part of the culture you want to lead, then you must start taking action... even if it takes one or two years to achieve.

Equally, if there is a gap in your team, it is never too early to start filling it. Even if you do not need that person for a year or two, start thinking about it now. If you can find the right person and have to get them on board earlier than ideally you would like to, that is a short-term financial pain that is well worth it. You may even find your plans come to fruition earlier.

You cannot make the progress you need to with the Infinite Cycle if you have the wrong people on board or gaps in your team.

It is best to start with a simple analysis of who you have now. Create a simple spreadsheet analysing each person's current performance against targets (their P-Score) and commitment to the organisation's purpose & values (their V-Score) – don't forget to include yourself (you will see my name below!). Simply score their performance against each of their targets out of 10 and their commitment to the purpose and your three values, and take an average of each. Then plot them on a graph similar to the one below. We call this the P-V Tool.

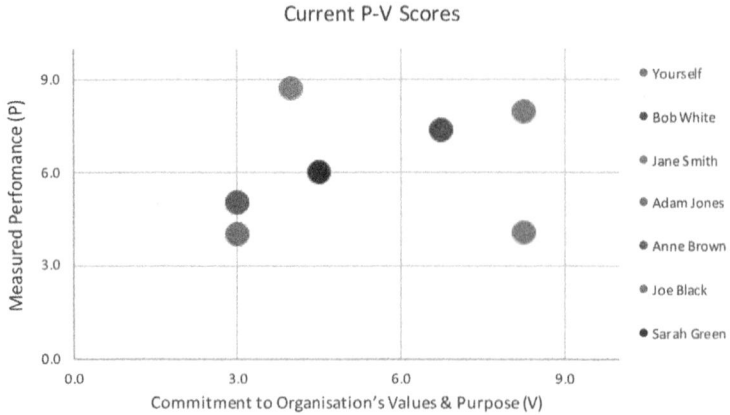

Then look forward a couple of years and decide what their potential scores might be, creating a graph similar to the one below. Do not share this with anyone from your team (for obvious reasons).

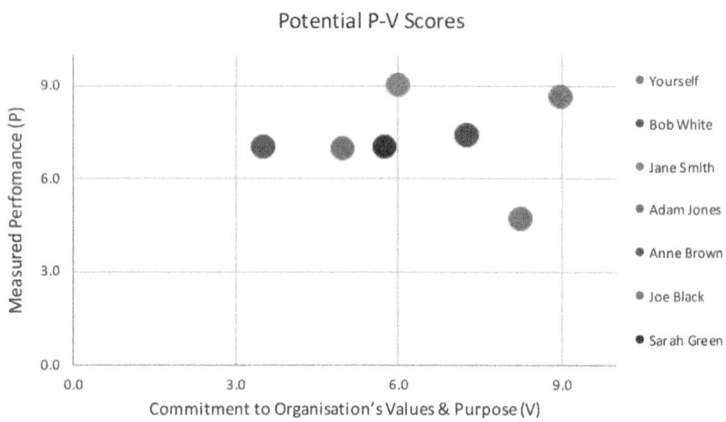

10: Right People

You are trying to ascertain who in your team fits into the following categories, looking at their potential a couple of years ahead:

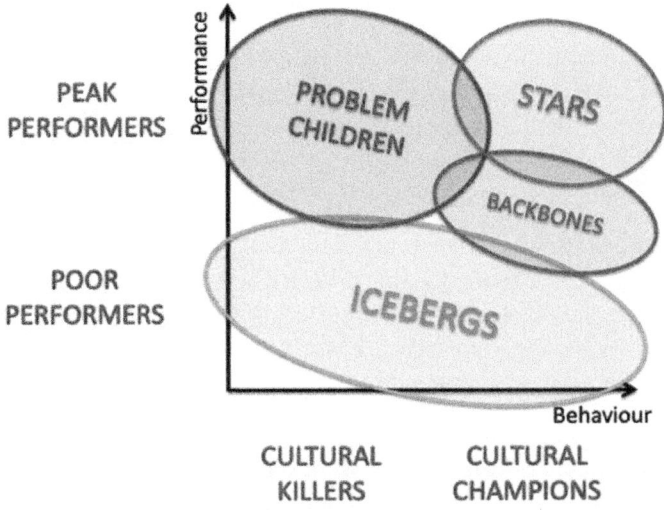

The Icebergs need to go. You have no faith in their future performance. Consult your legal team and try to remove them as soon as possible, preferably through some sort of instant deal. I would always advise against performance-managing people out of a business if it can be avoided. It is a long, draining process that often ends up costing in real terms the same amount as if you had taken action earlier.

The Problem Children need to go too. It just might take a while to implement a replacement plan if they are performing key roles. But you have no faith that they will change, so they will always be killing your culture and tolerating them will make a mockery of what you are trying to create as a team.

The Backbones need to be looked after really well. These are the core people who will be with you over the long term. Make sure you are giving them your full support and understanding their needs really well through exceptional one-to-ones (more on those in Chapter 13).

The Stars need to be treated specially. You need a development plan in place with them all and often may need to increase their remuneration or promote them earlier than you would like to. Ideally you want two or three who will be looking to take on your role when you move on. Be aware that it is natural to lose Stars too. The only organisations that manage to retain nearly all their Stars are those which are growing at such a rate that new layers of management and opportunities are constantly being created to run the organisation effectively. However, if you get the Infinite Cycle right, this could be you!

Now look forward five years and imagine what you will have achieved as a team by then. With the above changes made, who are you missing? Start recruiting them now. The process starts by asking your network who they know who fits the bill, and informally meeting with people. Research who is one or two degrees of separation away who you would love to have in your team. Meet these people when you can and check you get on with them.

Then when it comes to interviewing, which may be three to six months away, have a well-prepared process that 'peels back the layers of the onion'. Ask them for examples of how they have lived by your values or striven towards your purpose. Do not take their first answer. Delve deep and peel back the layers until you are sure they are genuine. You must avoid recruiting any cultural killers. If possible, invite them to events or for socials with the team prior to bringing them on board.

I cannot tell you how often organisations have dealt with getting the wrong people off the team and getting the right people on the team and simply regretted that they had not done so sooner: it is nearly every organisation that we have worked with. It just frees up so much positive energy to make progress and accelerate the Infinite Cycle.

The golden rule is pay more now to get rid of the wrong people and pay what is needed to get and retain the right people. Simple, obvious, common sense... but rarely common practice!

11 TOP Planning

It's all very well doing lots of thinking, figuring out what is going to happen in the future for your team and developing plans with your team on how to achieve it. But you still have to be able to summarise it and, referring back to Woodrow Wilson's quote, this is often going to take some time to be able to do so in a concise manner.

It is also really important that as leaders we take responsibility for pulling this together. It does not matter if you work for a larger organisation that has not articulated its plan. That is just the world we live in. Not perfect. In fact, very few large organisations manage to neatly cascade their plans from the top down. At some level of the organisation, someone has to make sense of what is imperfect information coming from the outside world and set a plan. The key is to insist that you will have it for your team.

A word of caution though. There is an old military adage that 'plans rarely survive contact with the enemy'. So, although it is hugely valuable to think ahead, set a vision and goals, do not ever get too wedded to them. You only have to look at the coronavirus pandemic to realise that things can change... often extremely rapidly. Whatever plans you come up with, the key is to regularly review them and update them. This whole process of regularly doing so with your team will prove invaluable.

Overleaf is the template that I would recommend you using. I call it The One Page (TOP) Planning Tool:

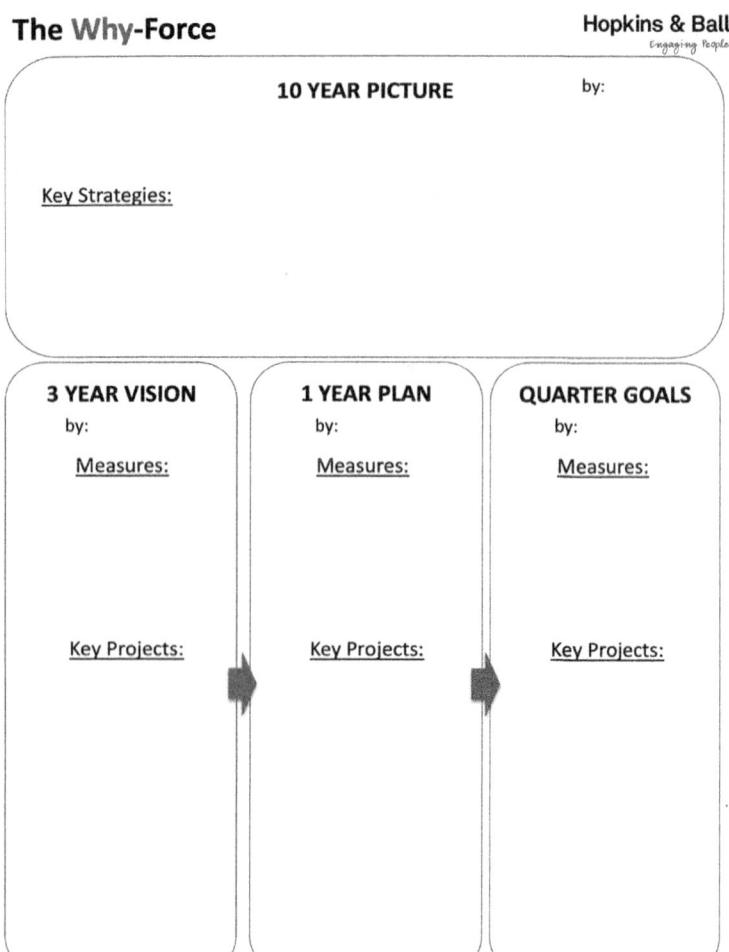

It helps to start with a very high-level, long-term view of where your team is going. I recommend calling it the 10 Year Picture. It does not have to be ten years. You could choose five or even three if your industry is very fast moving. It just needs to be further out than it would make sense to set specific goals for. Get your team together, pick a date, remind yourselves why you exist (your Why-Statement) and draw up a picture of where you see you team being by that date. Start with some blue sky thinking, ignoring the current reality or current constraints, and then come

11: TOP Planning

back to an agreed picture of where you feel as a team you could get to. Just keep it deliberately high level.

Once this is agreed, identify the key strategies you are going to have to adopt in order to achieve this. Keep them within three to six. This may seem like a very 'light' process, but in my experience it is enough. The answers will be within your team and, of course, this picture can change throughout the year as new technology, information and so on comes to light.

Here's an example of what it might look like:

---

10 YEAR PICTURE   by: 2030

£2.5m turnover, 15 retained key clients on pre-agreed packages of >£100k each. Customer Satisfaction rating of 95%. Employee Engagement Score of 85%.

Key Strategies:

- Retained Client Progression Project
- Launch of NPD24 product & service package
- Implement Customer Satisfaction Scores
- Full company TOP Planning & 1P121
- Full company Weekly 60 & monthly updates

Once the long-term picture is agreed, it is time to move to a more defined three-year vision. This does not have to be done in the same session; in fact, it is often better to leave some time to digest what has been agreed. Again, it does not have to be three years – you may choose two years, but unless you are an extraordinarily fast-moving industry, I would keep it at least two years out.

Set the date and then picture as a team where you need to be by then in order to be on track to achieve the 10 Year Picture (or your equivalent of that). Start by identifying the measures of success. It is best to keep it to between three and five. I would include one measure of employee engagement, one measure of customer satisfaction and between one and three measures of cash flow. Remember the Infinite Cycle.

Then think through the key projects that you will have to complete in order to achieve those measures and be on track to get to your 10 Year Picture. Look at the key strategies identified in the picture. Again, keep them in the region of around three to six key projects.

Once the three-year vision is agreed, simply repeat the process by thinking one year out and working out which measures need to be achieved to be on track. And then which projects or parts of the projects need to be completed by then.

Finally, repeat the process to set some goals for the next three months. I recommend picking a quarter, because it is a reasonable chunk of time to get things done in and to measure progress.

Agree this as a team, write it all up in TOP Planning format to give you something like the example below:

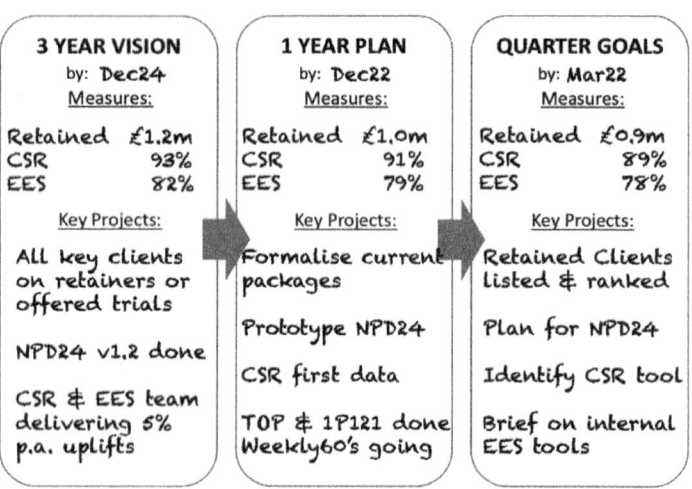

Finally, two key steps:

Step 1: Set the next meeting to repeat the process in three months' time. Put the meeting in everyone's diary. You can move it nearer the time, but it NEVER gets cancelled. You may choose to only lightly look at the longer-term elements of the TOP Planning Tool and do the fuller visioning exercise only once a year. But... you must examine and update this plan EVERY SINGLE QUARTER from now on.

Step 2: Make the measures live. Do whatever it takes to make sure that every single member of your team knows the status of those key measures and key projects all the time. Put them on a display, put them on people's desktops, tell everyone, every day about them. Whatever it takes. Make sure people are up to date and focused on them. Focus will mean they happen more often than not, and far faster.

12 The Weekly 60

To create a team culture of success, you need regular focus. As individuals, it is best to focus every single day, whereas in teams this is often better once every week. And for most teams, once a week for about 60 minutes is enough (hence the Weekly 60 or Weekly Go... if the 60 does not work for you).

The mistake that most teams make is to spend that precious time together as a team updating each other on progress. This is largely a wasted opportunity. If there are important measures of success and updates on key projects (those identified in your TOP Plan), they should be shared on a live basis. If things have cropped up during the week that could be solved by one of the team or a chat between a couple of the team members, then that should have already happened.

Your weekly time together needs to focus on two things:

1. Developing team culture, bonds and understanding of each other.
2. Solving the issues as a team that need to be solved as a team.

It should not be talking about the day-to-day responsibilities or frustrations – only about issues that affect the whole team or improve how the team work together. As you can imagine, it takes some discipline and effort to get into the habit of keeping to such a format, but the results and focus are well worth the effort.

The Why-Force for Leaders

Here's the format of that meeting that I recommend:

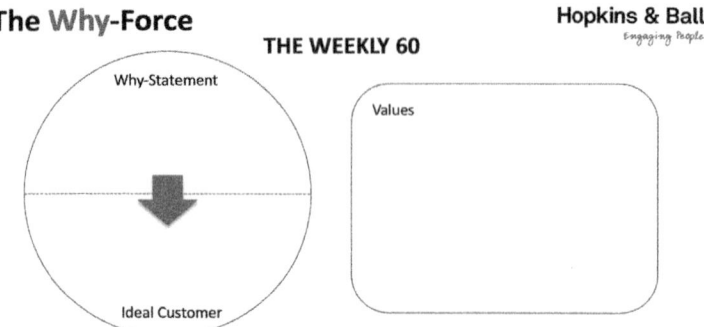

Phones to silent. Alarms set for 25 & 55 minutes

TIMINGS	AGENDA
START ON TIME (5 minutes)	'1VY Moment': each share **1** story related to the team's **V**alues or Wh**Y**-Statement
(5 minutes)	Update on ideal customers & colleague news
(5 minutes)	Confirm Agreed Actions complete (from Last Weekly 60)
(5 minutes)	Review Measures – add to Current Team Issues Log
(5 minutes)	Review Key Quarterly Projects – add any Issues to Log

Sharing & updates stops at 25 minutes when alarm goes off

(30 minutes)	3D (Define, Discuss & Decide solutions to Issues) - Priorities from Current Team Issues Log

3D process stops at 55 minutes when alarm goes off

5 minutes	Confirm Agreed Action Log
END ON TIME	End on time (or early) every time

At the top of your agenda, you won't be surprised to see a place to remind you to put in your Why-Statement, your ideal customer and your values. Try and put them on every standard document you use internally where there will be an opportunity to refer to them.

12: THE WEEKLY 60

To establish the discipline of this meeting, I suggest agreeing all phones go to silent and two of the phones are used to set alarms at 25 minutes and 55 minutes. It is going to be tough to get this habit established if this is not how you normally run your meetings. But, if you do not establish the discipline, you will not spend enough time focusing on one or two team issues. Time can always be filled. This time together should be viewed as gold dust.

You need to get people out of thinking about the day-to-day stuff, time pressures or current irritations that could easily distract them from the meeting. It is also important to get everyone to speak. So, ask everyone to share one (1) story related to the **V**alues or Wh**Y**-Statement in an **IVY** moment. Warn them in advance, and it is not a bad idea to keep a log of these. You can use this log as part of your reward and recognition scheme which we will come to in a later chapter. Do not accept ungenuine or repeated stories. Your team will quickly start to remember these instances and it will greatly accelerate progress to living by your values and for the Why-Statement.

EA Technology is a fantastic organisation focused on 'promoting the development of resilient, accessible, low cost energy networks globally, accelerating the transition to energy decarbonisation'. I have been lucky enough to work with them for a number of years and they were one of the first organisations to adopt what they called their 'Values Moment' at the start of meetings. They do have five values… so two too many… but very quickly this became a genuine process with stories being shared throughout the management team.

Next in your meeting, ask for any significant updates on ideal customers (do not let people talk about other types) and any significant colleague updates (new starters, people leaving, new qualifications, personal successes). If there is bad news, just share the facts. If there is good news, celebrate it.

Then, a really key part of what will create a culture of success. Very, very quickly just ask people to confirm that the actions (which you will have listed in a shared 'Agreed Action Log') from the previous week's Weekly 60 have been done. If not, express your disappointment (particularly if you did not already know) and spend NO TIME discussing the reasons behind it. Talk to the person after the meeting, but do not let them waste any more of their colleagues' time re-discussing this action which was agreed. Most actions that have not been done are symptomatic of people not feeling they were important enough. It sounds harsh, but accepting excuses will kill off any culture of getting things done.

The fourth and fifth stages of the meeting are to review the live measures and live updates on key projects (however you display them). This is not an update of what these are. That should be available to everyone all the time. It is a chance as a team to spot issues with progress and data and, if necessary, add any new issues identified to the 'Current Team Issues Log'. This is a log of all issues that you feel must be solved as a team, i.e. ones that you are going to solve in the Weekly 60 sessions or as a team later on. Each issue should be stated in the log and ranked from 1 to 10 in terms of importance. This will help you automatically identify which ones to prioritise.

How you store and display your Agreed Action Log and your Current Team Issues Log are up to your team to decide. They could be on a physical board if you meet in the same place, but I would recommend an electronic version of them linked to your project management software. Preferably in the same place as you show your live measures of success and live updates on key projects. A shared spreadsheet is a simple fallback position, but not recommended, as they are unwieldy for teams to use and for everyone to see simultaneously.

These first stages must be completed in the first 25 minutes (before the first alarm goes off). If they are not, stop anyway when the alarm goes off and just resolve to get through these stages quicker next week.

As a team, you now look at your Current Issues Log and simply determine which one (or possibly two) issues you will now turn the next 30 minutes to **D**efining, **D**iscussing and **D**eciding on solutions to (**the 3D process**). You may choose to allocate 20 minutes to one issue and 10 minutes to another one, but you must stick to this time.

12: The Weekly 60

After 55 minutes, the second alarm goes off and you simply add the agreed actions you have come up with to the Agreed Action Log before the meeting ends.

End on or before time, every time.

The huge benefits of this process take a large amount of discipline from you as the leader. But it is worth sticking to. Within two or three weeks, you will have created a hugely successful culture and a further acceleration of the Infinite Cycle.

13 1P-121 Tool

In some ways, this chapter is the simplest. But, you won't be surprised to read, as with all simple things, it is perhaps the most powerful tool you have in engaging your people. It is about giving consistent, quality one-to-one time to your team.

When you train as a coach, one of the first things you learn is that your job is to help the coachee raise their sense of awareness and responsibility: awareness of what their options are; responsibility in terms of taking ownership. If you help someone do this, it does not really matter how you go about it. However, in practical terms, it's best to have an attitude of being genuinely there for them, listening really well, asking questions to help clarify things, perhaps doing a bit of brainstorming of ideas and then getting them to shape their path ahead. Sales trainers refer to the old sales adage 'You have two ears and one mouth. Use them in those proportions.' Taking that a bit further, in a good one-to-one, and in sales too, use them in that order. Listen first. Then offer your input.

Before we look at helping people who report directly to you take ownership of their responsibilities and their plan, you need to be sure that you have been delegating what you can. So, referring back to the TOP Plan in Chapter 11 and re-looking at the Desire–Ability matrix in Chapter 7, firstly construct an organisation chart as overleaf for you and your direct reports.

The Why-Force for Leaders

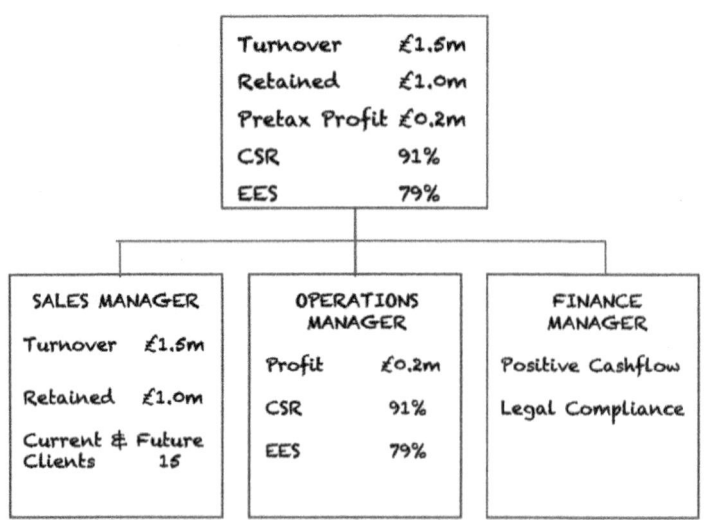

It should start with your key measures for your team, which ultimately you are responsible for, and then break down how parts of or those entire measures are delegated to your team. You might also add a few key functional responsibilities that individual members of your team have, such as completing one-to-ones with their own sub-teams, having an up-to-date quarterly plan or taking care of a compliance issues.

In an ideal world, you would be able to fully delegate every measure to members of your team. Take a moment to consider why you cannot do so. If it is people related, you might want to look back at Chapter 10 and reassess if you have the right people on board your team. It may be that certain measures or parts of those measures do need to remain with you, but be confident in the value you add as a leader and do not fall into the trap of feeling you need to have full responsibility for lots of measures. Ultimately you already have responsibility for all of them, but the role of the leader is to get your team to take ownership of them and achieve more than you could have on your own.

Below is the simple, one-page, one-to-one tool (1P-121 Tool), that we recommend using with each of your direct reports. If you work for a large organisation, you may have to also complete an

13: IP-121 Tool

appraisal or personal development plan once a year. These tend to be longer and more about completing the form, but use this one-to-one form anyway. It will only help you when it comes to complying with the corporate system... and you get the huge benefits from doing so every month in the meantime.

You fill it in together. It does not need to take a large amount of time. Usually 30 minutes is enough and, when you come together monthly to update it, often 15 minutes will suffice. Their name goes at the top and then add your team's purpose and values (these can be pre-filled on a standard form if you like). Then, sharing your team's TOP planning tool, which they should already be familiar with, ask them to confirm the measures and areas for which they are responsible. Hopefully, you will both have a good shared understanding of this.

The next phase is, very importantly, a 'listening phase'... two ears, one mouth, in those proportions and that order! Ask them to suggest what they would like their measured targets for each of their areas of responsibility to be. Generally speaking, this is for a year, but as you get more and more into the quarterly plan, you might revise this down to closer to a quarter. A good coaching question to help them define measurable targets is 'How would you know you were achieving them?'

You may need to suggest they are a little less ambitious or even more ambitious in their targets, but try where possible to accept their suggestions. We are programmed to take far more responsibility for those things that we feel we have autonomy over.

Once the targets are defined, ask them to self-assess their current level of attainment of living by the purpose, living by each of the values and achieving each of the targets out of 10. Remember that you will have already done something similar 'to them' when using the P-V Tool, so it is important that you clear your mind and let them say how they think they are doing. If they give themselves higher or significantly lower scores than you feel are appropriate, give them specific, evidenced examples of why you feel that they should reassess how they are doing. This process will allow you to get to assessed attainment levels that you both agree on 99 per cent of the time.

The Why-Force for Leaders

Name: Jerry Hopkins		Current (/ 10)	Hopkins & Ball Plan
PURPOSE			
Helping organisations create engaging, sustainable jobs		9	
VALUES			
1. Walk the talk		7	Daily reflection
2. Customer Fan Base		9	
3. Appreciate People		8	Rank relationships
PERFORMANCE			
Areas of responsibility	Measured Targets		
1. Turnover (Retained)	£125k (£80k) per month	7	Recommendation strategy in place
2. Pre-tax Profit	£0.2m p.a.	9	
3. Customer Satisfaction Score	91%	8	Review support organisations
4. Employee Engagement Score	79%	7	Fully implement Why-Force tools

It is then a case of asking them some simple coaching questions to develop a plan:

➤ What would help you get to +1?

➤ What is stopping you getting to where you want to be?

➤ What training or development might help?

➤ What experience do you need to have to help you?

➤ How can I as your line manager help you? (Could be mentoring/coaching.)

➤ What do you need to do more of or less of?

Again, it is really important that this is done as a listening phase. You can always input your suggestions once they have made their suggestions. Focus on agreeing a plan that they feel is *their* plan. It is so important that they have ownership of this. There is a line from Lao Tze, founder of the I Ching, that goes 'When the best leaders' work is done, the people say we did it ourselves.' A vitally important concept for positively influencing the Infinite Cycle.

Once you've put this together, both take a copy of the 1P-121 and book in your next one-to-one in a month's time. Never, ever cancel this. Only ever move it if necessary and always book the next one in at the end of your meeting to create a perpetual system.

Once a year or once a quarter (depending on the time frame for the targets), have a slightly longer meeting to redo the one pager. But, for the other meetings, you simply update the existing one, adding in small changes to targets, updates to how much they are living the purpose and values, tick off parts of the plan that are complete, etc.

The key thing to focus on is the conversation (and not the form) and their sense of responsibility and ownership for what comes out of the conversation.

Interestingly, at EA Technology, they combine their system with a very simple, yet powerful 360° feedback system that we run for them. At Hopkins & Ball, we focus on helping improve employee engagement scores, but a second measurement we have in place is the 360° leadership scores (in other words, how the employees of that business rate their leadership team). Over the years, EA Technology – which already scored above 70% on this rating – has raised this to a highly impressive 85% by making a few changes (I refer back to the P-V Tool), but also upskilling leadership skills in the specific areas defined by the 360° process. I mention this as it is a powerful example of combining one-to-ones with 360° feedback. It goes without saying that their Investors in People (IIP) scores have increased impressively in the same period.

Simply do this with each of your direct reports... forever! And, VERY IMPORTANTLY, insist that all those who report to you who have direct reports of their own do the same. You would want to see proof that each of your direct reports who line manages people has completed the P-V Tool, has a TOP Plan and has up-to-date one-to-ones... and that they are doing so for the managers who are reporting in to them.

14 Engaging Jobs

The Japanese car manufacturer Toyota was one of the first companies to fully embrace continuous improvement or Gemba Kaizen... Gemba being workplace and Kaizen loosely translating as continuous improvement. It is well worth taking the time to study what they did, but a couple of practices stood out to me. The first was that the managers always had to assemble the first car of a new design. The second was they would draw a 'Gemba Circle' in the production area. Managers had to regularly go and stand in that circle to better understand what was going on.

There is an old adage, 'Don't ask someone to do a job you'd not be prepared to do yourself.' Stating the obvious, this does not mean in leadership terms that you would want to do it forever. Fortunately, we all want different things from our work and our lives, take satisfaction from achieving different things and have different strengths and weaknesses.

My son, Ted, was lucky enough to get a job through an agency (so nothing to do with me) with one of our customers, The Contact Company. Their business is in a traditionally hard-to-engage working environment of contact centres, replying to calls, emails and live chat on behalf of their customers. However, The Contact Company go to great efforts to engage their employees with their customers – if you are lucky enough to pay them a visit, you'll see they are set up in branded customer teams – but they are also far better than most of their industry at connecting their agents with the live situation and how they are doing. The result is that Ted, and most of their agents, are engaged in doing a great job for their customers. They also have a great structure of team leaders and coaching support and give their agents the best tools, using software to make their job as non-repetitive as possible.

The Why-Force for Leaders

Netflix is an organisation that only started life in 1997, but has been hugely successful. At the core of their culture is what they refer to as F&R: Freedom & Responsibility. What it means is that where possible, employees are given the *responsibility* to deliver certain metrics and the *freedom* to achieve them how they like, including choosing where and how they work to a large extent. Those who do well thrive. Those who do not achieve their metrics leave.

As we covered in the last chapter, a key factor in engagement is also the support of your line manager through the one-to-one process. So, when assessing jobs in your team, you should consider if you have given people the right Freedom, Responsibility & Support or FRS.

The challenge is to eliminate jobs in your organisation that are dull, repetitive and in a poor team environment and make sure every job has FRS in place as much as possible. It sounds like an unrealistic challenge, but it is not. If a job is just very dull and very repetitive, it can probably be automated (or at worst outsourced... I know this is passing the job to someone else, but another company might be better at automating or making it more engaging). You simply do not want to have these types of role in your organisation. They lead to problems and low engagement. And you want to be sure you are maximising FRS.

So, starting with your job and your direct reports, start to plot each role in your organisation on the chart below. You will need to estimate the Engaging Job/Team Design Rating and FRS Rating (both out of 10).

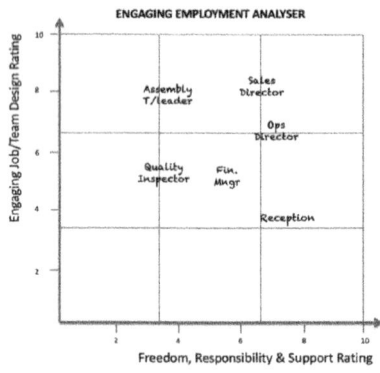

The FRS Rating is simply a reflection of how well the outputs expected from the role have been clarified, how much autonomy is given to the person doing the role (compared to how much could be given in practical terms) and how well the one-to-one process is working to support the role. Zero would mean none of this has been done and 10 would mean it is being done as much as practical within that role.

The Engaging Job/Team Design Rating is a bit more complex. The best way to think about this is to imagine someone you love doing that role (hopefully not the person currently in it!). Given that person is undertaking that role for, say, eight hours a day of their life, would you be happy that the person you love is doing so for that amount of time? Chances are that if not, it should have a lowish ranking.

A formal way to approach this ranking would be to go through these questions:

1. Has everything possible been done to remove any dull, repetitive elements to this role that could be replaced with automation, reduced to a minimum or eliminated?
2. Where repetition is necessary, are there rotations with other members of the team, say every 30 minutes, so people get variation in their role?
3. Is the role designed to be as safe and ergonomically as sympathetic as it could be?
4. Is the team set up to be a fun, playful, high-energy environment as much as possible?
5. Is the work environment as pleasant to work in as physically possible?
6. Do the team members really engage with the values and purpose of the team?

Now simply pick the worst three roles you have ranked within your team and book yourself in to be in that role for a day, if you possibly can. Or at least ask a line manager to do so. Get into that Gemba Circle, build that car, find out what it is like

The Why-Force for Leaders

and take action to eliminate the 'bad' or less than perfect jobs from your organisation. Commit to working with everyone, so you only have engaging employment. It does not matter if this means eliminating roles. All engaged organisations grow with the Infinite Cycle, so you won't be getting rid of people (unless they don't fit with your purpose and values).

15 Icing the Cake

Generally speaking, if you are doing monthly one-to-ones, Weekly 60s, have a shared TOP Plan, are not employing people who are not culturally aligned and are striving to eliminate non-engaging jobs, you will have a highly engaged team already.

A bit more communication, recognition and team bonding is really just the icing on the cake. But it is icing you may as well have!

During the Covid lockdown of 2020, one of the businesses we are lucky enough to work with, Howorth Air Technology, asked us to facilitate a live session during which Jim Liptrot, their fantastic managing director, and all his fellow directors were to be on screen. Jim delivered a briefing, one or two of the directors added some of their news and then it was opened up to questions. The session was recorded in case anyone missed it.

They have been hugely successful and over 70 per cent of the staff have consistently attended the live briefings which have continued on approximately a monthly basis ever since the first one; one was even dedicated to a particularly long-serving and dedicated employee retiring.

It has kept everyone briefed, enabled them to ask questions and also see the whites of the directors' eyes. They have simply focused on solid **communication**, showing their 'ICE' values of Integrity, Collaboration and Excellence.

What is interesting though is that for the previous five years, there had been nothing stopping this happening. The technology already existed. But, as many other companies were, the focus was on delivering these briefings face to face (often with all the expense of travel, venue hire, catering, etc). It turns out it did not need to be and it has been far better to have regular, essentially free-to-organise, monthly briefings and Q&A sessions. They only last 30 to 45 minutes, but are priceless.

The Irish playwright, George Bernard Shaw once said, 'The biggest problem with communication is the illusion that it has taken place.' It is very easy to slip into the mindset of thinking everyone knows what is going on… but they don't.

So, are you as an organisation doing this? If not, just do it! Do it as a minimum once a month for the whole organisation that reports into you and try and encourage that it is done for the wider organisation beyond your own areas of responsibility.

It is worth noting that there is also some value in doing some inter-departmental networking. Dow Schofield Watts have 'Una Validores' as their purpose statement (the only company we work with to have one in Latin). It translates as 'stronger together as one'. They are a hugely successful firm doing financial corporate advice, due diligence and recovery, among other services. During the Covid lockdown of 2020/21, they started hugely successful quarterly networking sessions where people from different parts of the business came together to generate ideas on a particular topic.

It really pays that, once a quarter, the regular briefing is followed by a short 30-minute to one-hour session which randomly puts those taking part into groups of three or four to talk through ideas on a topic. Someone needs to facilitate this using the breakout room function on MS Teams or Zoom and debrief the outputs from the group. Examples of topics could be:

➤ 'How can we improve the results of our employee engagement survey?'

➤ 'How are we going to be working in the future?'

➤ 'How can we generate more business or ideas through inter-departmental connections?'

and so on.

The ideas generated will be of benefit at the time. The connections created will generate even more value longer term.

There is also value in the once-a-year get-together in terms of having fun as a whole organisation and meeting people from different areas, as this creates warm connections which leads to further collaboration and ideas. So, if your organisation can afford to do so, it is still worth holding these sorts of events occasionally, but NOT to cover off the basic communication. That still needs to be done monthly.

The second layer of icing is the **values-based recognition scheme** which we referred to in Chapter 9. Simply capture all the stories shared in the IVY moments of the Weekly 60s. Select the top ten examples that most show the values or purpose of your organisation and send out a simple poll to everyone to vote for their top three. There are loads of easy-to-use voting software options. You could even use the poll function on your live monthly call on MS Teams or Zoom or whatever platform you use. This ties in nicely with announcing the winner on that call. Make the prize quite small (the equivalent of around £20)... anything bigger can create envy and have the opposite effect! Then ask the line manager of that employee or team to choose something bespoke to them and present it to them in the following month.

Again, easy to do, so if you are not doing so already, just do it.

The last layer of icing is **team bonding**. If you are getting things right, a lot of bonding will be naturally coming from the success and achievements you are making as a team. Doing things well together and striving to be the best naturally has this effect.

However, there is no substitute for the richness of bonds that forms from also doing something fun and completely non-work related (apart from the people involved) together.

It does not have to cost very much – although it helps to have a small budget of something like £200 per person for the year – and it does not have to take up much time, but it is best to be flexible on this if you can.

The best timing is fairly logical. If you as a team are working to the TOP Plan and effectively trying to deliver a 'project' every quarter, the best time to do some team bonding is at the start of that quarter. So, aim to do something four times per year.

The best way to organise what to do is form a small committee per team. Often just three or four people is best (in a small team, it might just be everyone!). They need to be volunteers and they need to be committed to finding out what everyone else would like to do before coming up with their own ideas. Again, easy for them to do with simple surveys. One question in the first survey needs to include finding out if people are prepared to do something outside of working hours (in most organisations this will not be possible for everyone, so be ready to accept doing this in work hours... it's well worth the investment).

The social committee for each team then, understanding the budget and what people would like to do, organises the session. It needs to be done at least two months in advance and take holidays into account. Often someone might miss one session, but they need to make sure that no one misses two in a row.

Examples of free team-bonding sessions are going for a walk together or organising a quiz (online or offline). Examples of sessions needing a small budget are going for lunch together or booking an escape room (online or offline). Once in a while you might push the boat out and do a more expensive team-bonding activity, but do not make it the expectation ... otherwise you will not do it when there is any sort of financial pressure.

Again, if you are not doing so, just do it. The default way of doing the above requires no budget and only a small commitment of time.

Given icing is quite low cost (in fact it can be zero cost), you might have your icing and eat it!

16 Simply the Best

To start this final chapter, it is appropriate to reference what Cicero, Blaise Pascal, Benjamin Franklin, Mark Twain and Woodrow Wilson have in common.

In Roman times, this quote was assigned to the orator Cicero: 'Cicero excused himself for having written a long letter, by saying he had not time to make it shorter.'

Then in 1657, Blaise Pascal published a collection of open letters entitled *Lettres Provinciales* and within them he notes, 'I have made this longer than usual because I have not had time to make it shorter.'

A century later, in 1750, Benjamin Franklin composed a letter describing his ground-breaking experiments involving electricity and sent it to a member of the Royal Society in London: 'I have already made this paper too long, for which I must crave pardon, not having now time to make it shorter.'

Then in 1871, Mark Twain wrote to a friend, 'If I had more time, I would have written a shorter letter.' This is the most heard-of version of what is effectively the same statement.

Finally, there is an anecdote from 1918, which I mention in Chapter 8, when Woodrow Wilson was asked about the amount of time he spent preparing speeches. His response was illuminating, and worth repeating here: 'That depends on the length of the speech,' answered the President. 'If it is a ten–minute speech it takes me all of two weeks to prepare it. If it is a half–hour speech it takes me a week. If I can talk as long as I want to it requires no preparation at all. I am ready now.'

The Why-Force for Leaders

The point is that it takes some time to simplify things. You have probably found this with your Personal Why and possibly your Team's Why.

Unless you just naturally get to these quickly, it actually takes a large amount of self-discipline to get to this level of simplicity.

You then need more self-discipline to focus on it. Remember the story of Bill Gates and Warren Buffett being hosted by Mary Gates. As a leader, you need your own personal focus and then to keep the team focused by having a clearly updated quarterly plan (TOP Planning tool) and using the Weekly 60 tool. This allows you and your team to proactively do more of what achieves your Why (focusing on the 20 per cent) and to eliminate the 80 per cent that does not (your 'avoid-at-any-cost' or 'not-to-do' list) – see Chapter 4.

It is about choice. And recognising how much choice you and your team really have.

More discipline is required to honestly access the people in your team (using the P-V Tool), to delegate the things you should not be doing (the Desire–Ability Matrix) and to sustain the monthly one-to-ones (1P-121 Tool) throughout your whole organisation.

Howorth Air Technology, EA Technology, Kimpton Building Services, Compass Minerals, DeepStore, Active Business Communications, Dow Schofield Watts, Garic – and indeed all the organisations that we have been lucky enough to help improve employee engagement at over the years – all have leaders who bring consistent, sustained levels of discipline to how they inform and engage the people who are lucky enough to work for those organisations. Importantly, it never comes across as a boring, rigid system. It comes across as leaders genuinely caring about the people in the organisation... because they do.

Finally, do not forget to Ice the Cake with more discipline about monthly communication, a value-based recognition system and quarterly team-bonding activities.

With all that the world throws at you as a leader, it is very easy to be knocked off course.

To a certain extent, once you have defined your Why-Statement and values of your team, everything else can be managed through your diary. Make sure the next session is in your diary for referring to all the tools. Then never, ever delete these sessions. And always schedule the next one at the end of the previous one. That way, they always happen, even if occasionally a week or so later than originally planned.

Most leaders then find the bigger challenge is maintaining discipline at a personal level.

You will know if you have already formed the habit of daily thinking time. Just two to five minutes per day. If you have not, then you need to question your desire to really create the change you set out to make by reading this book. Remember, Mohammed Ali and his hate of training. If you have not established this key habit, but you do still want to make this change, put it in your diary (again!), tell people you are doing it and create the quiet space to do so. All you are trying to do is to take one action per day towards your Personal Why and schedule in one Beacon (to help sustain your energy).

It really helps to have some measures in place relating to the most important changes you want to make and to record them somewhere. And do not forget the power of telling others (and if possible pulling together a team) or putting in place all the key elements of learning a new skill or habit (do not forget the cheerleaders).

For most of us, when we look in the medium to long term, luck does not really exist. It is about the quality and discipline of your thinking and how committed you are to taking action that for the most part will determine how successful you are compared to what you really want... your Why.

Use the Why Force to your benefit. It is free. It is easy to use. Yes, it requires discipline, but what it brings to you and your team is well worth it. Remember Jerry Barber: 'The more I practice, the luckier I get.'

Good luck... or rather... good thinking!

Acknowledgements

There are really two groups of people I need to acknowledge without whom this book would not have come to fruition.

Firstly, my family and particularly the most wonderfully talented and insightful person I know, my beautiful wife, Caroline. Over the years, she has given me the confidence and support to run my own business that has allowed me in turn to help hundreds of organisations and thousands of leaders. A lot of the tools and techniques in this book have been jointly developed with her and she has (sometimes even politely) pointed out the shortcomings of ones that did not make it. At the same time, she has been running her own amazing business, Love Presenting, helping thousands of leaders (and some grooms and best men!) give fantastic speeches and talks. All that she does to support myself and our three wonderful children, Ted, Barney and Emma, has given me the time to focus on the business and this book. To Ted, Barney and Emma, I hope that I have not been too grumpy a dad while I was writing this... love you!

Secondly, all the wonderful businesses and leaders that I have had the privilege to work with and who again have been instrumental in helping develop the Why Force. Particularly:

- Jim Liptrot, Adam Ainslie, Tom Ford, Jason Marchant, Claire Fenlon & Carlo Rava at Howorth Air Technology
- Dave A Roberts, Mark Spawson, Lynne Sampson & Mark Wilding at EA Technology
- Richie Kimpton & Tim Davis at Kimpton Energy Solutions
- Mark Boyle & Chrissy Petrou at Active Business Communications

The Why-Force for Leaders

- Gordon Dunn, Chris Heywood & Gary Sinclair at Compass Minerals & DeepStore
- Nicole Burstow at Dow Schofield Watts
- Mark Albiston at Garic

There are of course hundreds of other leaders, businesses, friends and supporters who have contributed to this book...thank you all.

Work with Jerry

Jerry's work is dedicated to helping leaders create engaging sustainable jobs around the world.

He works with whole organisations to tailor the tools and techniques of the Why Force to their needs so they can be implemented across the whole organisation and facilitates Boards of leaders who are committed to sharing their knowledge and ideas with each other.

He also works with individual leaders to coach and mentor them through how to apply the Why Force approach to themselves and their teams.

If you would like to explore the possibility of working with Jerry, please contact him at **jerry@hopkinsandball.com** or visit his website **www.hopkinsandball.com**.